For Sue, with whom
I love working & playing —
    Margot

© 1970 by Dillon Press, Inc. All rights reserved

Dillon Press, Inc.
Minneapolis, Minnesota 55401

Standard Book Number: 87518-020-5
Library of Congress Catalog Card Number: 73-115872

Printed in the United States of America

The photographs are reproduced through the courtesy of Dayton's, pp. 9, 43, 75; Donaldson's, p. 33; Jerome Liebling, pp. 39, 85; and, the Minneapolis School of Art, p. 49.

For William and Sandra, whatever profession they choose, and for Harold, who may prefer fashion to the law.

TABLE OF CONTENTS

Introduction 1
Fashion Is 5
How Do I Prepare for a Fashion Career? 13
How Much Education Do I Need? 19
So You Want to Be a Fashion Writer 25
Some Prefer Fashion Advertising 31
Fashion Shows Show Fashion 37
The Designing Male — and Female 41
How Does a Designer Learn? 47
It's a Model World — or Is It? 53
The Excitement of the Marketplace—Retailing ... 63
A Store Is Many Things — and Many People 73
The Manufacturer Is All — and Then Some 83
And We Have Not Mentioned 91
Quiz Yourself 95

A word of thanks to all those in and out of the fashion world who were helpful in the preparation of this book. Special thanks to Bernadine Morris, Mildred Custin and the staff at Bonwit Teller, Edie Shepherd and Dayton's, and those at the Minneapolis public schools.

INTRODUCTION

WHEN I WAS ASKED to write this book on fashion as a career, I was delighted. How great to share with you my feelings about fashion and to tell you what a rewarding and ever-changing field it is, in all its phases. How wonderful to suggest a career in which each job leads to another, even more interesting and varied than the one before.

What an adventure to start out in retailing, perhaps as stock help, then go on to merchandising, advertising, journalism or some other form of communications like television or radio, designing, even to marketing, franchising, display, computer programming, chemistry, law or psychological testing—and still never leave fashion.

Then I had second thoughts. How, in a world so perilous and ever-changing, can one individual over thirty (how much over thirty I will not say) tell thousands of young people what they should aspire to? Will they listen and read? I hope so.

You see I know that any information that is set down today for the young professional of tomorrow may become somewhat outdated. What looks so grand and imposing today might be Dullsville tomorrow.

Yet, I know, too, that the old clichés about hard work and success are just as true today as they were for your grandparents.

I know that the medium is the message and the message is old before it leaves the typewriter and that what you must plan for in this computerized era is CHANGE!

You might switch careers several times before you retire. When you, today's students, are in mid-career, there will have been professional revolutions. But again, how exciting to know that you can do many things in many places during your professional lifetime.

Fashion is important to everyone but not everyone knows how to make a little know-how go a long way, financially and emotionally. You may want to use your know-how to help others keep themselves attractive by volunteering in mental wards or poverty pocket neighborhoods.

Now, remember that everything you read in this book is really an outline for you to fill in according to your own needs. Keep in mind that computers are taking over routine office jobs, and sometimes even factory jobs, and that you must be prepared to be a versatile worker in that part of fashion which interests you.

Learn everything; grab knowledge as though it were your lifeline, because it is.

You have been told time and time again that the worker with the most education makes the highest income. This is usually true, but remember as you read this book that the amount of money you make in your lifetime is not nearly as important as the satisfaction you get out of your career. So be sure to choose the fashion world only if it fits with your interests, your talents and your life schedule.

True, you should listen to your parents and to your advisors, but always listen to your own drummer. This is your life and your career. Enjoy it.

Margot Siegel

Fashion Career Memo

From: Mildred Custin, former Board Chairman
and President
Bonwit Teller, New York

To: Young, career-minded students

DURING THE PAST quarter of a century the fashion business has grown so in stature—and expanded so greatly—that it is now one of the most fascinating and far-reaching forces in modern industry.

To start out in fashion today is to embark on a glorious adventure, an adventure into a cosmos of color, form and fabric, and into a world of people who create, produce, buy, sell and influence fashion.

The fashion world today needs the inspiration, the

imagination, the determination and the dedication of many people. It is a big business that involves and utilizes every possible talent, skill and interest. And, in every phase, there are essential and exciting jobs.

Open your eyes, your minds and your hearts to the many opportunities that are available. Aspire, if you will, to be a great designer, but remember that the creative mind and the talented fingers of an artist need not be confined to the designing of clothes. You can find expression and acceptance in the field of fabric design, in fashion display and advertising, even in store design.

Merchandising is another area that offers excitement and challenge and unlimited opportunity for advancement and achievement.

If I knew the secret to success in the fashion world, I would gladly tell it to you. Frankly, I do not believe there is a secret formula. But, if there is a secret weapon, it is a strong sense of ambition and an unquenchable desire for attainment.

CHAPTER 1

Fashion Is...

ALMOST EVERYTHING THAT happens in this world in some way affects fashion and is affected by it. After the astronauts, both Russian and American, began to conquer space, suddenly "the space look" became fashion. Historically, wars have caused hems on skirts to go up or down; World War II and its aftermath were the inspirations for the famous Dior "New Look," when skirts went down, down, down and waists were suddenly cinched once again.

One author seriously predicted recently that rising hemlines would mean rising stock prices. Another, just as seriously, predicted the opposite.

Current student riots are certainly as memorable for the fashion look of the rioters as for their demands. Close your eyes and reconstruct the look of a militant student. Suddenly you will see a beard, or long hair, beads, Indian bands, all kinds of hippie adornments. Young people who demand Black Power enforce their ideas by flaunting untamed Afro hair, wonderfully flamboyant native African garb and animal-tooth necklaces to prove to a hostile world they have an identity different from that of the Caucasian. They have made their point, and influenced fashion radically.

During a recent show on television, a young militant commented, "You will remember how long my hair was, but will you remember what I said?"

The Beatles, who reached their first fame as a singing group, suddenly became the spokesmen for a whole generation that has called itself "mod" (for modern), a generation that has played up kookiness and the ye-ye look to the hilt, and still has had a serious purpose.

If your school has a dress code establishing what you may wear and what you may not, it too is part of the fashion world.

So, when you pick up a book like this whose purpose is to tell you all about fashion as a career, perhaps the first thing you want is a real definition.

What is fashion?

The Random House Dictionary of the English Language has many definitions of *fashion*. It may be "a prevailing custom or style of dress, etiquette, procedure, etc.," or, "a conventional usage in dress, manners, especially of polite society, or conformity to it."

Among the synonyms for *fashion* are: *mode, fad, rage, craze.*

One of my favorite dictionary definitions is "fashion is that which characterizes or distinguishes the habits, manners or dress of a group." That definition takes care of squares, hippies and yippies, as well as stewardesses, soldiers, sailors, jet-setters, fathers and mothers and all others.

Because even the dictionary does not quite know how to characterize fashion, it also throws in such words as: *shape, cut, pattern, frame, construct, mold, suit* and *fit*. These, as you can see, belong to dressmaking and tailoring—only one facet of fashion and one which we shall discuss in other chapters.

You can tell this definition business becomes a bit stuffy when even the biggest dictionary on the market can not quite come to grips with *fashion* as a word.

Maybe the time has come to listen to the words of a lady who was one of the really creative and original fashion designers America has produced. Her name was Claire McCardell, and though she has been dead a number of years, many less-inventive designers are still copying her ideas. Miss McCardell was a refreshingly nonserious writer as well as a designer, and in a book called *What Shall I Wear?* she defined fashion like this: (Incidentally, you see here a good example of one person working in several phases of fashion, designing and writing.)

"Fashion is elusive. Some people have it without knowing it. Consider the peasant girl who knows how to tie her kerchief. Consider the art student who doesn't—even though she is majoring in fashion design.

"What you do with fashion makes it fashion.

"Fashion is contradictory . . .

"Fashion breaks rules. Be flexible, it warns you . . .

"Fashion is change."

This last definition, that fashion is change, is not only Miss McCardell's idea. Several retailers and designers told me the same thing when asked for their interpretation. Fashion lives on obsolescence, which means making something out-of-date.

FASHION FIGURES

You have all been in school long enough to know that any book that attempts to inform must throw figures at you to show how important is the subject under study. So, after the definitions come the figures.

Because fashion is a such a volatile business, it would be better to skip figures: they change so quickly. But let us toss in a few, mostly because they are rather impressive if one is thinking of entering that field.

The fashion business even in the early 1960s was already the third largest in the country, exceeded only by food and steel, with a sales volume of more than thirty-seven billion dollars!

In 1968 Americans spent five-hundred million dollars on, would you believe, neckties? And as a famous fashion historian, James Laver, curator *emeritus* of London's Victoria and Albert Museum, points out, "The necktie is already on the way out as far as fashion is concerned."

This is a good time to make a point I hope you will remember throughout this book. Note in how many different ways fashion is a career. Mr. Laver is a man who has made a lifelong career for himself as a historian on modes of dress. He has written many fine books on the history of styles and is quoted frequently throughout the world by experts and laymen alike. He has lectured extensively, has assisted designers and

manufacturers, and has achieved many honors, using fashion as his starting point.

Back to the facts and figures. We Americans are devoting a steadily increasing percentage of our annual income on adorning and dressing ourselves. For instance, in 1967 we spent a whopping thirty-five million dollars on apparel, excluding shoes. That means that more than seven percent of all our family expenditures were on some form of clothing. Fashion, then, is big business.

But there is more to fashion than figures and the business approach. It plays a real role in our lives; old or young, we derive real pleasure from being well-dressed, and also in helping others express themselves through what they wear.

There is a good feeling in looking attractive whether one is on a date, job hunting, or just walking down the street; fashion is a morale booster.

Psychiatrists know that lack of interest in our own appearance sometimes is a signal of mental illness. A disturbed person often becomes sloppy, with unkempt hair and wrinkled clothes.

Those of us who choose fashion as a career become the ones who set ideals of taste for all those statistics we are talking about here.

APPAREL AND ACCESSORY FIGURES

A bulletin for the Small Business Administration states that apparel and accessories for women, misses and children represent one of the most important industry areas in the United States. Upwards of 350 thousand workers are employed in more than ten thousand establishments in the women's outerwear industry alone.

Another seventy-seven thousand make children's clothes in approximately two thousand establishments. In addition, thirty-eight thousand workers are employed in the corset and allied garment industry, sixty thousand in the knit goods industry, twenty thousand in the millinery industry and ten thousand in the fur industry. Thousands more are employed in the neckwear, costume jewelry, handkerchief, umbrella, belt, handbag, leather glove and fabric glove industries. And let us not forget the bride and her very special needs.

Next we think in terms of related or allied industries —the vast wool, cotton, silk, linen and man-made yarn producers, the textile manufacturers, and the converters who supply the fabrics.

Want more? There are the plastics manufacturers and fabricators who supply plastic products (you can even be a chemist in fashion), while trimmings, buttons, laces and knit goods originate somewhere else. Think of the metal body jewelry being worn as clothing now, making metals part of fashion, too.

To complete the cycle, uncounted thousands of retail establishments, ranging from the smallest boutiques to the largest chains of stores, employ people to sell these apparel items and accessories. These products will be bought by consumers like you and me and by radio, television, theater personalities, often to be worn in their work as well as for their personal use.

Are you convinced? You can imagine how vast the fashion industry is when you realize that in New

York alone more than two million people are employed in the combined fashion industries.

If you are a facts-and-figures person and want to read more, you or your teacher should write to the Small Business Administration in Washington, D. C., and get all its apparel bulletins; they are fascinating in their own dry way.

CHAPTER 2

How Do I Prepare for a Fashion Career?

THE CHAPTER TITLE is the one question asked most frequently by students who are thinking of entering the fashion field.

Instead of using the experiences of many young people who are preparing for this career, let us pick one. It could have been a young man, because so many boys will choose fashion as their world. For now though, let us select a sixteen-year-old girl named Ginny. This attractive young lady lives in a midwestern city (after all, not all fashion-minded people live in New York or California, though many do) and attends high school. She is a nearly perfect example of advance preparation for a chosen career.

Ginny, now a senior, hopes to go into merchandising, though she may switch to another area of fashion later. What she is accomplishing however, would be just as valid if she were thinking of designing, writing or modeling.

At the time this book is being written Ginny has been chosen one of seventy-five finalists, from a group of

160 teenagers around the country, by Bobbie Brooks, a manufacturing conglomerate (a word you should look up as it is becoming more important in business all the time) in the teenage range.

Ginny represents a large department store, part of a retailing conglomerate (there it is again), and is competing for a scholarship and a trip to New York, that will be awarded to twelve finalists.

Already she has visited a local manufacturer's representative (a salesman in a given territory) to review and evaluate the firm's current line. She has interviewed a copywriter and a buyer from the store that sponsors her in order to learn about each one's function within the retail organization.

Finally, she has followed a piece of merchandise from the time of purchase by the store through the different departments such as advertising, display and public relations to its sale on the floor (not literally: "on the floor" means the department that does the selling).

Now Ginny will read and criticize a teenage magazine. Next she will be in charge of a fashion show at her school; this will be her final project. For the show she will choose the models and pick the Bobbie Brooks fashions her schoolmates will parade; she will also coordinate the show and serve as commentator.

Whether she wins or loses the Bobbie Brooks contest, Ginny will have gained a very important look into the world of fashion at many levels.

She is also a well-rounded person in other extracurricular activities. She has worked on foreign student exchange programs and is thinking of tutoring students in beginning algebra. She is on the student council and is a member of a school precision dance team that is raising funds to perform in Europe. She has participated in local theater and last year was a member of a department store teen board. She also has been a salesgirl at the same store as well as at a neighborhood drug store. She loves to ski, both on snow and water.

Upon graduation Ginny will attend college and concentrate on a merchandising program offered at the school of her choice.

Now you can see that Ginny typifies the kind of person who will make it in fashion. Her interests are broad; she is keen and alert, and she is looking for ways to get an early start on her life's work.

Other Ginny's throughout the country are applying to retail stores and teen boards of magazines and stores. They are working weekends as stock girls or models, sometimes assisting in a designer's workroom as well. There are so many other fashion-oriented jobs, some of them even in home economics classrooms.

One beautiful young girl I know was a winter carnival queen several seasons ago and has now found her place in a large store as a training assistant. She has become an expert on running complicated movie and slide projection equipment, as well as tapes and other tools of the fashion-training trade.

Economist Sylvia Porter reports that 85 percent of all teenage girls sew more than eighty-two million items a year; a large group of you do this sewing for friends and relatives, and get paid. In fact, you might seriously consider going into the needle trades where there is a great shortage of talented people who sew.

A vocational school background is helpful here, though on-the-job training is always provided. Sewing is also a wonderful trade for those who must work in sheltered workshops.

While the girls are out doing all kinds of jobs getting ready to enter the fashion world, after finishing their schooling, the boys are not at all idle. Male students sell, do stock work, assist in window and interior display, help bookkeepers, designers, cutters, markers, pressers or production people in a manufacturing plant. With men's clothes leaping into the fashion arena after a century of stagnation, the opportunity for men in fashion is growing rapidly.

Some boys even spend summers as touring salesmen, or work with production engineers.

THE IN-SCHOOL PROGRAM

Many in-school programs gear you toward the fashion and retailing world. Young people in all fifty states are members of Distributive Education Clubs of America, a school group which develops future leaders for marketing and distribution. Boys and girls who belong to DECA chapters often spend part of their school time actually working in retail stores, also learning from important retailers in their own area.

The nonprofit organization has a national leadership conference, a national advisory board and also sponsors competitive events.

"If I hadn't been a member of Junior Achievement when I was in high school, I wouldn't be working in the retail field now." Speaking is a young man who is now a stock head in a major department store and a volunteer advisor to teenage Junior Achievers.

JA is a national organization with a program to help high school students learn more about the American free enterprise system. Organized into miniature corporations, these teenagers run a business with the help of advisors. They sell stock in their companies, manufacture a product, market it, and take either a profit or a loss, all through their own performance.

To show the scope of JA and its interest nationally, here is a quote from the April 29, 1969, issue of the *New York Times*. The article is datelined Washington:

> "A one dollar investment in each of two Junior Achievement firms has returned a total profit of forty-nine cents to President Nixon.
>
> "He received a check yesterday from William Leadens, president of a now liquidated firm in Minnesota run by high school students. The firm made aprons and scarves.
>
> "Another check for one dollar and ten cents was presented to Mr. Nixon by Patricia A. Young, seventeen - year - old secretary - treasurer of the First Junior Achievement Bank of Minneapolis. The bank, too, is liquidated.
>
> "Mr. Leadens and Miss Young were representatives of a nationwide economic program in which high school students organize and manage businesses.
>
> " 'I congratulate you on a good report,' Mr. Nixon told Mr. Leadens, 'and you can come down and fix our budget.'
>
> "Mr. Nixon bought a dollar's worth of stock in each of the two firms when he was in Rochester,

Minnesota, during the Presidential campaign last year."

Other service clubs like 4H have various programs tying in with school work.

A new direction in early career planning at the pre-high school level has been undertaken in Kansas City and Minneapolis, and perhaps several other cities. These cities have run Job Fairs in their local auditoriums.

The public schools and Chambers of Commerce (and in the case of Minneapolis, the Urban League) are in charge.

At the Job Fairs, local businesses including retailers and beauty schools have manned booths in which employees tell students how and what to study in order to enter their businesses. The government competes with private industry to woo students, incidentally. Isn't it nice to be fought over?

Perhaps your city has such a Job Fair in the offing. Check with your school counselor or local Chamber of Commerce. It is fun and interesting to talk to someone who is already established in the career you wish to enter.

CHAPTER 3

How Much Education Do I Need?

THIS IS THE QUESTION the second largest group of students ask about a fashion career. As I pointed out in the introduction, yours is the era of the computer, of space travel and enormous advances in technology.

Perhaps some of you will still make it big, like Horatio Alger, without a college degree or some specialized school training. Still, there is so much career competition that you should get as much education as possible.

If finances are a problem in your family, talk to your vocational counselor, for there are many scholarships available in fashion design and retailing. Merchandisers and manufacturers donate funds to local vocational schools, design schools and colleges. Many retailers offer tuition scholarship to children of their employees.

As you can imagine, we called upon and wrote many top fashion executives during the writing of this book. Although several indicated that imagination and drive were primarily what they looked for in prospective employees, most agreed privately that some kind of college background is almost mandatory for young people hoping to go up the executive ladder.

The kind of college schooling was not too important. Mentioned were liberal arts and merchandising degrees, as well as marketing and advertising and journalism backgrounds.

Because fashion's definitions are so sweeping, a liberal arts education is always a help, as is a study of the humanities. If these terms are vague, again check with your counselor for definitions.

If you want to go into the really creative end of fashion such as designing, sketching or photography, read the chapter on fashion design carefully. But, even here, the word is, "Have some general education in your background."

For those who do not quite know where they are going in the way of a career (and how many of us that category includes!) specialization can wait until after a B.S. or B.A. degree is earned. A high school diploma, however, is a must for even the least intriguing of fashion jobs today.

Because fashion is truly international, with the lead coming from France, Italy, Spain, Great Britain, America, and other countries, a knowledge of at least one foreign language is a great asset. Foreign fashion personalities will have more respect for you if you are not a one-language American. If you can afford it, it is also good to have gone on student tours abroad before you begin serious work. Having been abroad changes your whole outlook on the world—you know we are all "one."

Even successful executives do not always know the exact advice to give a beginner about schooling. As one young woman put it, "Some people have told me to get a four-year college degree in merchandising. Then I am supposed to get on a store executive training squad or spend a year at a school like Tobé-Coburn. (Note: This is a two-year fashion school in New York, founded by the late Tobé, a fantastic woman who scoured fashion markets and advised thousands of store clients around the country. She was a legend in her time.) Others tell me just to get a liberal arts degree."

The consensus then, as far as education is concerned, seems to be to get as much schooling as you can. Even graduate degrees are not too much for those who want to hit the top in our competitive society.

A good way to find out about your chances of obtaining employment in the fashion field of your choice is to consult with your counselor. You or your counselor can write to the United States Department of Labor in Washington, D. C., and ask for various bulletins in the Employment Outlook series. They cost from five to fifteen cents and are worth every penny.

You in New York should check on the Fashion Institute of Technology in Manhattan. It is under the program of the State University of New York. Out-of-towners, too, can attend this well-rounded fashion institute for a higher fee.

Fashion as a career is for both the creative and the business minded, for male and female alike.

Avon Lees, the male director of the all girl Tobé-Coburn School for Fashion Careers, Ltd., says, "There are few fields where there is less competition with men for those jobs to which women aspire." He continues, "There is no field where they can make a greater contribution because they are women. There is no field that offers more executive jobs to more women for more money than does the fashion field. . . ."

Although more women are entering more areas of the fashion world, the opposite is also true. Men have been successful in many jobs, mostly in the sales and buying fields formerly held by women. There are even male editors of women's pages with some daily newspapers.

An ability to work with the hands may be just as valuable as a brilliant mind, and sometimes the two come together in a successful combination.

You should also be interested in the world and how people live. You should follow innovations in the arts and in music to really make it in fashion, but there is one more thing you must know, and we come to it now.

MASTER THE MACHINE

We have talked about computers and other electronic wonders of the age, but in fashion, as in almost any other profession, there is one machine that must be mastered — the lowly typewriter. Typing know-how opens many doors professionally and is an invaluable aid to you personally, all the way up the career ladder. Even though in later life you may have a battery of secretaries at your disposal, there are times when you will want to set down your own thoughts—and in private. True, there are dictaphones and tape recorders for immortalizing one's own words, but they are not the same. And if you are going into advertising, publicity or any of the other communications media—radio, television or movies—your typewriter is like your right hand, or left, as the case may be.

Now that communications have sped up so, it is also a great help to know how to run a teletype. Be sure, too, to learn either conventional shorthand or develop a method of your own, as I did. You will be amazed how often in your working life you will wish to take notes quickly, either on the margins of a fashion show program or at a lecture or rewarding group meeting.

It is important to be handy with all office equipment —copiers, tape recorders, even film projectors and the like. They are being used more and more everywhere, even in the classroom, as you may have noticed.

CHAPTER 4

So You Want to Be a Fashion Writer...

THE BY-LINE (that's what journalists call the way a writer is given credit in an article or story) on this chapter should read "by Bernadine Morris." The reason: she wrote most of it.

This subject was really never meant to be chapter four, but because it so beautifully repeats what I tried to tell you in the last chapter, it is inserted here.

Before we get on with fashion writing as a career choice you should really know something about Mrs. Morris and her background; then you can better appreciate the weight her words carry. She is a most efficient lady, one of the better fashion writers in America, and certainly one of the most literate. She is also the mother of two children, not yet in their teens, and currently is a reporter on the women's page of the *New York Times,* one of the most prestigious newspapers in the world. Previously she was an editor on the fashion staff of *Women's Wear Daily,* the bible of the fashion press. *WWD,* as it is known in the trade, is a daily tabloid newspaper that gives all the fashion news, even the gossip, that interests workers and executives in the fashion and retailing world. Lately it has become so peppered with jet set and celebrity names and rumors that fashionable consumer-type ladies are just as eager to read it as are those in the trade. It is a reading must if you want to be part of fashion. You need not always, however, completely believe everything you read. (*WWD*'s greatest editorial fault is that it virtually ignores the center of the United States in favor of the East and West coasts, not recognizing that fashion news is made everywhere.)

The world of fashion is great for making lifetime friends, and a true friend helps when you need him—or her. Case in point: The way Mrs. Morris came through when I asked her to help young people thinking of going into fashion writing.

Here are her thoughts on the subject:

"So you want to be a fashion writer. You're lucky. A generation ago you would have been regarded as one of those hopeless misfits who wanted, say, to be a missionary to Mongolia. Was there really a pressing need for the work to be done? Was the desire to perform it so great it couldn't be conquered?

"Sure there were fashion writers. They tended to be in their eighties, had been on the job for at least half a century, and were so pleased with their work they showed little sign of leaving it. The opportunities, to put it mildly, were few.

"Strangely enough, things have improved. They have improved a great deal and in lots of directions.

"The field of fashion itself has expanded. A generation back, the women who were interested in reading about fashion were considered a limited crew who couldn't get their minds to function on any topic more complicated than the placement of a hemline. A flighty lot.

"Today a healthy interest in fashion is not necessarily a sign of a negative I.Q. Why, even men are beginning to express interest.

"With the flowering of men's concern about clothes—noticeable three years ago and picking up speed ever since—the fashion field itself has doubled. Then there's the fact that for women it's no longer confined to a snooty few. There is fashion at all levels, right down to the little children, who have their own ideas about rings for the fingers and flower-patterned panty hose for the feet.

"There is fashion in home furnishings, too, if you want to expand the field even further. What it all means is that fashion writing is as valid an occupation as, say, bookkeeping or teaching school, and for lots of temperaments, it is a good deal more fun.

"So, how does one go about getting into it? As with so many other things, a good liberal arts education is as strong a beginning as you could wish for, with as much arts background as you can fit in. And not necessarily fashion art. Byzantine art is just as useful. So is a study of the Impressionists, or Gothic cathedrals. It's your sense of aesthetics you're developing.

"Literature courses, history, anything that contributes to your cultural background will be useful. If you are exposed to and friendly towards French, by all means cultivate it. You might like to travel to France.

"There are some complimentary skills that might come in handy to anyone concerned with reporting fashion. They are (1) The ability to sketch. Fine, if you can do it with style, but OK, too, if you can just convey an idea of what you have seen, even if nobody's going to see it but yourself. (2) The ability to use a camera. Chances are greater that you could produce competent photographs than that you could learn to do professional sketches. Very little fashion reporting these days is done by words alone. (3) Shorthand—whatever system you prefer—including one you made up. This is mostly a convenience for the writer, taking some of the tedium out of notetaking. It was necessary for all journalism graduates when I was in college, and I considered it boring, but I must say I've found it a help. (4) Typing. This is a must. Beyond discussion. If you don't want to learn to type, forget about writing professionally.

"I have been considering newspaper reporting in making these notes, but it is hardly the whole field."

OTHER OPPORTUNITIES FOR FASHION WRITING

"There are opportunities for fashion reporting in many stores, even though the job itself may have another title like, perhaps, fashion coordinator. Still, it will involve a certain amount of viewing, describing, and analyzing clothes.

"Many buying offices, large fabric houses, and other organizations in the fashion field have a constant flow of reports moving between them and their clients. The production of these reports requires the same skills as newspaper reporting."

FASHION VOCABULARY

"What about a special vocabulary of fashion terms? Forget it. There isn't any need for it. A martingale is a little belt, but there's nothing wrong with calling it a little belt. Technical terms just produce turgid prose. The whole trick with fashion writing, as indeed with any writing, is to be as lucid and lovely as possible."

Nobody could tell it like it is any better and be more to the point than Mrs. Morris. Her writing is just as lively and lucid as she would want yours to be.

She also answers once again the question of whether a specialized fashion school is necessary. Her conclusion: "If you want to find out how clothes are put together, or if you want to learn to make your own, sure. But if your aim is to write about them, just sharpen your powers of observation, practice your writing and cultivate your memory. These are the skills you will need."

One last word about *Women's Wear Daily*. Any of you thinking of going into fashion should start reading it as soon as possible in order to get the flavor of that world; also some of you may work for one of its bureaus around the globe, or you may even go into the New York office to start your writing careers there. Others have. *WWD* is a tough teacher, but a good one.

For many, fashion writing is only the start. You may go on to become editor of one of the major glossy fashion magazines such as *Vogue, Harper's Bazaar, Mademoiselle,* or *Seventeen,* for instance. Or you may want to work for magazines like the *Ladies' Home Journal, McCall's* or *Good Housekeeping.* Other possibilities include the women's pages of local newspapers or major papers like the *New York Times*. Remember, too, the great publication jobs such as art or article editor of the fashion magazines.

Some of you may prefer going into advertising departments of stores or buying offices, or becoming copywriters in large or small advertising agencies, or even going into training departments to train others. We will touch on these other fields as we discuss retailing and manufacturing more fully.

More and more good fashion writers, by the way, also double as writers in general fields — the old versatility bit again.

CHAPTER 5

Some Prefer Fashion Advertising

IN THE LAST CHAPTER we talked a lot about fashion writing and barely mentioned advertising and its sister, fashion publicity.

All of you have seen fashion advertising in newspapers, magazines and in booklets that come with your parents' monthly bill statements. Even billboards occasionally carry a fashion message.

What you may not know so much about is the advertising agency where all these ads are planned, or a store advertising department where again the plans are made, the art is completed and the whole promotion is started on its way.

In an advertising agency, of course, there is a president or director who heads the operation. He or she has a group of executives who plan and have overall supervision. Then copywriters write the text of the ad. Artists prepare the illustrations and layout specialists put copy and illustrations into the most attractive and eye-catching arrangements possible.

There are the administrative and technical workers who see that the ads are reproduced well and the salesmen who must sell the advertising space in publications or on the radio or television. The publicity writer works with newspaper or magazine editors and gives them stories on the advertiser's product.

In a small agency, one person may do everything, and perhaps some of you may one day own such an agency, and specialize in fashion accounts. A large agency usually has someone for each job.

Advertising managers head advertising departments of agencies, department or specialty stores, or manufacturing companies. A manager may work with advertising agencies or handle everything himself. He or she will be responsible for special sales brochures, display cards and other promotional materials.

Advertising managers of newspapers, such as fashion trade papers or consumer publications, are concerned chiefly with selling advertising space. In a television or radio station, time is sold.

Account executives handle relations between clients (the people who buy time or space to advertise their fashion product or service) and the agency. These account executives must know how to write copy and handle artwork, though the actual work is in other hands.

Advertising copy writers do the real writing, gather information and figure out the psychology that will make you and me buy the product.

There are other people at work on the agency level, such as media directors, production managers, research directors, marketing directors, and artists and layout men.

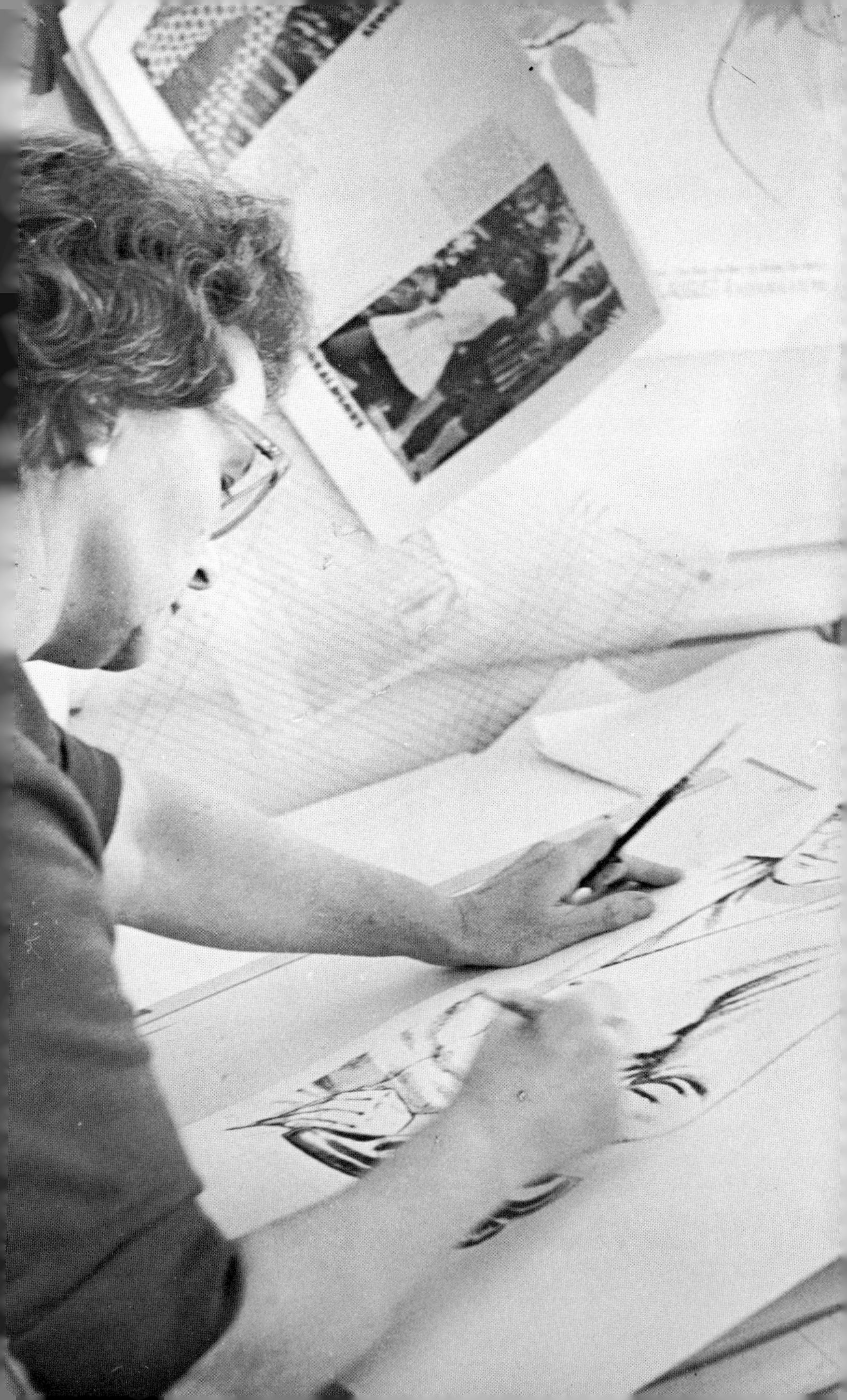

We will not go into all their jobs, but if you are interested in learning more of this part of the fashion world, again I direct you to the Occupational Outlook Report series, this time on advertising and public relations.

Usually the highest starting salaries are paid by large advertising firms recruiting college graduates, with lower salaries in the small agencies and stores.

You should realize, however, if you decide to go into the public relations, publicity or advertising side of fashion work, you must love quick changes, and also get a big kick out of constant activity and meeting a deadline daily.

On just one day, if you work in a store for instance, you may have to plot out a television commercial, think about a movie to be made for your department, a newspaper ad, a magazine ad, a direct mail circular for an upcoming sale. On that same day you may have to handle details for a visiting celebrity and arrange television and radio interviews for that person.

You need more than just talent to handle a schedule like that. Besides eating your Wheaties and your vitamins and getting a good night's sleep, you have to be highly organized, have good judgment as to which job is most important in your daily plan, and be able to work on your own without constantly asking someone else's opinion or help.

In fact, if you have developed good study habits in your schoolwork schedule, you will already have prepared yourself a bit to go into the business world.

In a publicity or advertising job, as in any job for

that matter, you must be able to get along with your bosses as well as those lower than you on the professional scale. You must enjoy other people, be willing to listen as well as talk. Also, temper is out!

True, some big names in fashion advertising and publicity have come so far they feel they can afford a bit of temper, and that may be one of the rewards of fame. However, if you want to be truly liked, you will never be big enough for tantrums.

In copywriting, whether for newspapers, commercials, direct mail, movies or billboards, always remember you are exercising a skill. You have to love words and love to play with them.

WHAT EXPERIENCE HAVE YOU HAD?

Many of you have asked how you can get that first job since an employer always asks, "What experience have you had?"

Your best bet is to have a good resumé of what you have done in the way of writing. (A resumé is necessary for any phase of fashion work as a matter of fact, so just adapt these ideas to the area of work you choose. For example if you are looking for sketching work, bring sketches, etc.) A resumé, by the way, is a written record of work you have done, perhaps on your school paper, for a neighborhood children's paper, anything that sounds impressive. It also lists your education and vital statistics, as well as your name, address, and telephone number. Along with your resumé, you might work out an idea for an advertising company on a product that you have dreamed up.

Another way to show off your writing ability is to

compose a letter to the advertising or publicity director of the agency or store that interests you as a place to work. Be sure your spelling and grammar are correct and that you use proper titles and spell everyone's name correctly. Check this beforehand with a quick phone call to the firm's switchboard.

It is not as easy as you think to be literate. When I was publicity director of a large museum, I advertised for an assistant. Graduates from top universities and colleges applied for the job, but the majority could not spell or put words together correctly. Also some who could spell and were good writers could not type.

One young lady, who could do all three rather efficiently, decided she would not take the job after I explained to her that, because our staff was small, we also did chores more menial than our titles would indicate. All of you should be aware, too, that any job, even at the professional level, has its share of dirty work that must be done—cleaning up before important visitors and that kind of thing. If you must be catered to, do not enter the copywriting or publicity world, or any phase of fashion, for that matter. The jobs are glamorous, varied—and sometimes beneath your training.

CHAPTER 6

Fashion Shows Show Fashion

"WHEN IS SHE GOING to write something about fashion shows?" That question is being asked by some of you by now. Fashion shows are glamorous and fun and an important way to show fashion, so let us explore them.

They can be filled with information, far-out and exciting as those presented by the New York Fashion Group for its own professional members or they can be simple and presented on the selling floor of a dress department. Most shows are somewhat in-between.

In department or specialty stores, shows are assembled by the fashion coordinator (if there is one) and staff. The display department contributes the "pizazz" and showmanship to the fashion show.

The past year or two there has been so much attention focused on multi-media that the idea of the show has changed. Now there is great emphasis on unusual lighting, on mixing movies or slides with **live** models and on wild, wild music, sometimes taped, sometimes live.

Different stores want to project different fashion images, so it is important that the fashion office, the display department and the advertising, publicity and current events departments meet and decide "who we are" and "what we want to say" in fashion.

Naturally, budgets are set up for shows, and the coordinator and staff decide how many productions there will be, and what kind.

There may be fashion shows for the store staff to alert them to what is new. Others are for career, college, bridal, teen, designer, and fabric departments. Again, some are on the floor, others in the store's auditorium or on a specially built stage somewhere.

Country clubs, service clubs, and auxiliaries often present shows, usually planned by a store. The store hopes thereby to sell merchandise. Also, many stores show fashion throughout the lunch and dinner periods in their restaurants or tea rooms.

The person in charge of the show (usually the fashion coordinator, or the publicity director in a smaller operation) must book the models, decide where the show will be held, meet with other store personnel, hire musicians if they are needed, decide what type of merchandise will be used, and work with buyers.

Naturally, a close check must be kept on all garments and accessories to see they are returned in good shape. Models must be helped dress and undress and the show must be publicized beforehand.

We talked earlier about the fact you must be un-

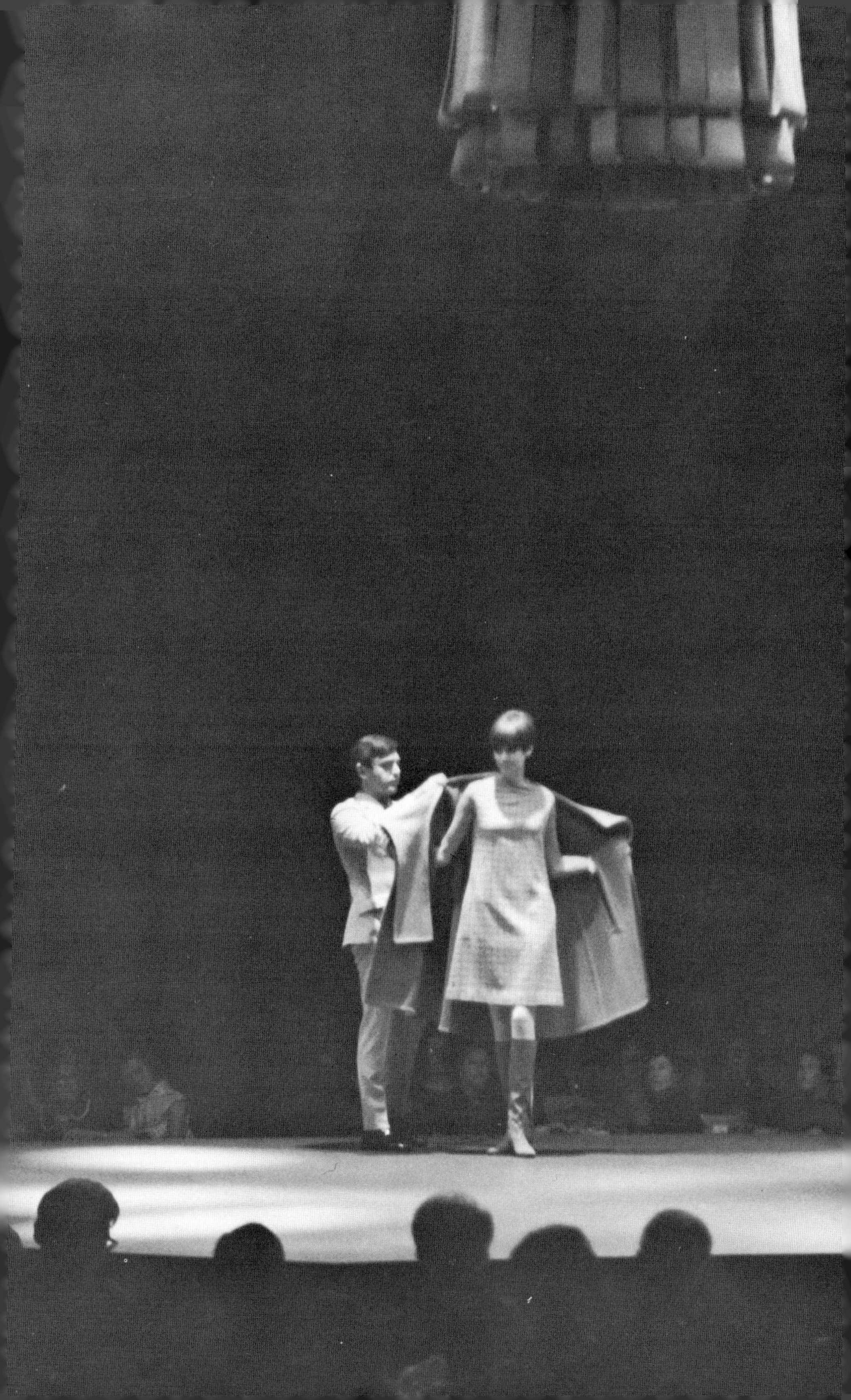

flappable and ready to do all kinds of tasks. This is especially true in fashion show production. You may end up dressing models yourself; you may have to scoot around looking for accessories; you must be sure no tags or petticoats are showing. You have to be strong, as you will nearly always end up carrying lots of merchandise and props back and forth. It is tough, demanding work, but again, very rewarding —if the show is good and the audience is pleased.

All the educational tools we talked about earlier are a help if you want to get into show production. You should have worked in a fashion office, or as a sales person. Some theater courses are not such a bad idea, either. It all gets back to design and the other fashion basics—most people get into fashion show production by accident and luck, by starting somewhere else in fashion or publicity.

CHAPTER 7

The Designing Male —and Female

IF WE WERE TO DO a free-association test on careers, and ask what word you associate with "fashion," many of you would automatically answer, "modeling." Another large group would specify, "designing."

Fashion design has long been considered one of the glamour professions for both men and women, and certainly it is one of the first professions. Eve probably started it with a fig leaf after meeting Adam.

You may remember from the Bible that after Adam and Eve ate of the tree of knowledge their eyes were opened, and they realized they were naked. At that point they sewed fig leaves together (enter the needle?) and made themselves aprons. Thus was designed the first miniskirt.

Man has always been concerned about getting adequate covering. Anthropologists, scientists who study man, are convinced that man first covered himself more for adornment than for reasons of keeping himself protected from heat or cold.

Psychologists explaining the origins of dress nearly always list these three reasons for its existence: (1) the craving to beautify oneself, (2) seeking to cover oneself for protective reasons, (3) modesty.

The history of dress is fascinating and we could go on about it for many chapters. We could discuss the use of animal skins and the discovery of the scientist, Darwin, who found people using red cloth for ornamentation rather than keeping themselves warm. We could tell about the beginning of the clothing industry, and how it evolved from shirtwaists. We could give you the history of the garment unions in America, and even tell of the Triangle Shirtwaist Company fire.

But these are all things you can look up for yourselves in history books. They make great term papers.

It has been said that fashions change, but fashion remains the same.

Anatole France, a famous nineteenth century French author, wrote: "If I were permitted to choose amongst the collection of books which will be published a hundred years after my death, do you know which one I would choose? Not a novel in this future library nor a book of history. I would simply take, my friend, a fashion magazine to see how the women would dress a century after my decease. And these furbelows would tell me more about future humanity than all the philosophers, novelists, preachers or scholars."

The most famous designers have usually been male, but there are more women designers.

Among the ladies, the French Gabrielle "Coco" Chanel has always been a trend setter. Even now, though she is over eighty, she designs a new collec-

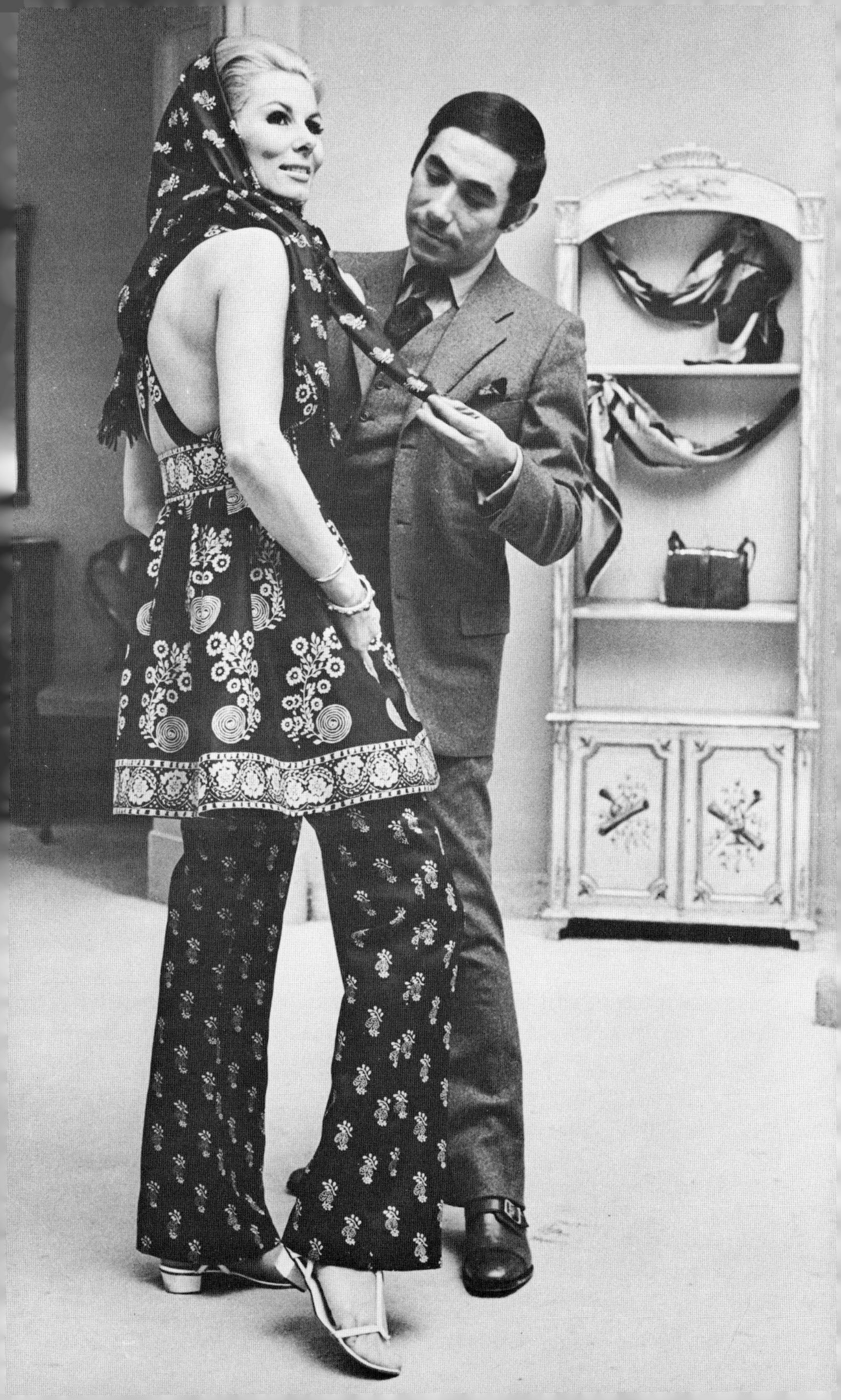

tion each season. She taught us to dress with ease and taste. The "little Chanel suit" is still a part of every woman's fashion dream.

Among male designers in America, one of the most creative was the late Gilbert Adrian. He designed for the great movie stars of the '30s and '40s. Look for his name on the movie credits when you see old movies on the late, late show (not on school nights, of course).

There have been many successful men and women designers and manufacturers who are very good at copying and adapting French, Italian, Spanish or American styles, but we cannot consider these people true creators. They are clever, however, and well paid.

Remember the tremendous variety open to you in the design field. You may find your place as a designer for young women, older women, fat women, short women, the handicapped—or for the same categories in men's wear. You may want to design for children, or to create accessories, fabrics, millinery or furs. You may have your own design studio and design for many manufacturers, each of them using your name. You may go into franchising, with your name and designs used in ways you never imagined (for better or worse).

Some of you may want to use your design know-how by working for a pattern company like *Vogue* or *Simplicity*. True, you may design or adapt, but you may also end up as a fashion coordinator, going around the country to fabric and department stores and working with home sewers.

If you are an excellent needle worker, as well as being creative, you may even go into private dressmaking or a small custom dress operation. Even if you just concentrated on fixing hems, there would be plenty of work.

A friend in the field who has had a long career in various phases of fashion and fashion design points out that you, as a budding designer, must have technical and production know-how—then you will never want for a job in the apparel industry. She says, "It is difficult to imagine a really successful designer without it."

I would like to add that in this day of multi-media talk it is interesting that famous artists have turned their talents to stage design and have been most successful. They understand the extravagant uses of color and use this talent to their advantage. Who knows, the designer of the future may design for everyday wear, for the stage and screen—and may even do all the sets, the lighting—and even write the plays or movies. We are coming to that. More and more it is the person who is versatile and does many things well who makes a name.

A new concept of merchandising for a successful designer is the boutique. Here you can sell your own designs in your own fantastically decorated shops.

By now most of you know that the majority of fashions designed in the United States are shown and manufactured in New York City on a street called Seventh Avenue. New York may be where most of the news is, but there are also important fashion centers in California, around the Los Angeles area; the Middle Atlantic states; Dallas, Texas; Miami, Florida; St. Louis, Missouri; Chicago, Illinois; Minneapolis and St. Paul, Minnesota; and, yes, Honolulu, Hawaii.

Minneapolis is known as the heart of the outerwear area (storm coats, really) and Honolulu specializes in those wild patterned men's shirts, muu-muus, and lately those swim suits and sportswear everyone is wearing.

Perhaps by the time you are ready to design there will be new apparel areas, especially in the South. More and more companies are moving there.

Perhaps you will be the designer who will open up still another part of the United States as a fashion center.

You all know that Paris is a fashion design center, and that Italy and Spain, as well as the Scandinavian countries are coming up fast. Yet nearly every country has a big apparel manufacturing center. You could become a designer anywhere—even Hong Kong or Tokyo. Fashion is truly worldwide, and design talent could be your passport.

CHAPTER 8

How Does a Designer Learn?

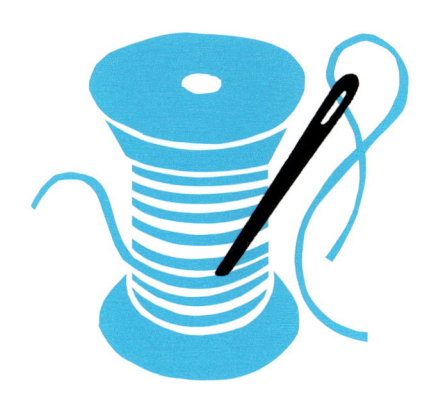

MANY TOP DESIGNERS feel that a young person entering the field today must have a minimum of two years' training after high school in specialized design before going out into the work world.

True, some of the big names made it without formal training, but it is still a good idea to attend a reputable fashion or trade school. However, even then you must be willing to learn and expand your horizons.

A beginner should learn as much as possible about fabric, cutting, the best use of a pattern and grain of material, fit and darts and seam binding and shoulders and zippers and buttonholes. Also, today's student must learn the properties of all the different synthetics and miracle fabrics and how they should be handled. A trade school will teach you all of the above, but on-the-job training is still the best experience.

You can learn about the fashion industry from some top executives in an excellent little book put together by The Fashion Group, Inc., called *Your Future In the Fashion World,* published in 1960—or from some designers in *Your Future in the Fashion World as a Designer,* published in 1963. They are already somewhat dated because fashion moves so quickly, but they have much to tell you not only about design, but how to handle yourself while job hunting and other good things to know.

Incidentally, no matter what phase of fashion you enter, learn about The Fashion Group, a group of women executives banded together all over the world "to the end that those engaged in the field of fashion may better serve themselves and the public at large."

Although that quote sounds a bit stuffy, Fashion Group members tend to swing. Their headquarters is in New York City and you can check around to see if your city has a regional Fashion Group of its own. If so, from them you can get information on fashion job possibilities in your area, and perhaps even get a fashion design scholarship. Many local Fashion Groups, which are nonprofit, raise money for this purpose. The top women in fashion in each city usually belong and will be eager to help you on your way.

Perhaps they will even let you be a guest at one of their meetings or may invite you to one of their fashion shows, which are always novel and exciting.

Most Fashion Groups sponsor a career course at least every other year, and this is something you will surely wish to attend. Also, after you yourself have been a fashion executive for three years or more, you are eligible for membership. Then, whether you are in Chicago, Melbourne, Paris, Tokyo, Mexico City or Honolulu, or lots of places in-between, you can check with fellow members.

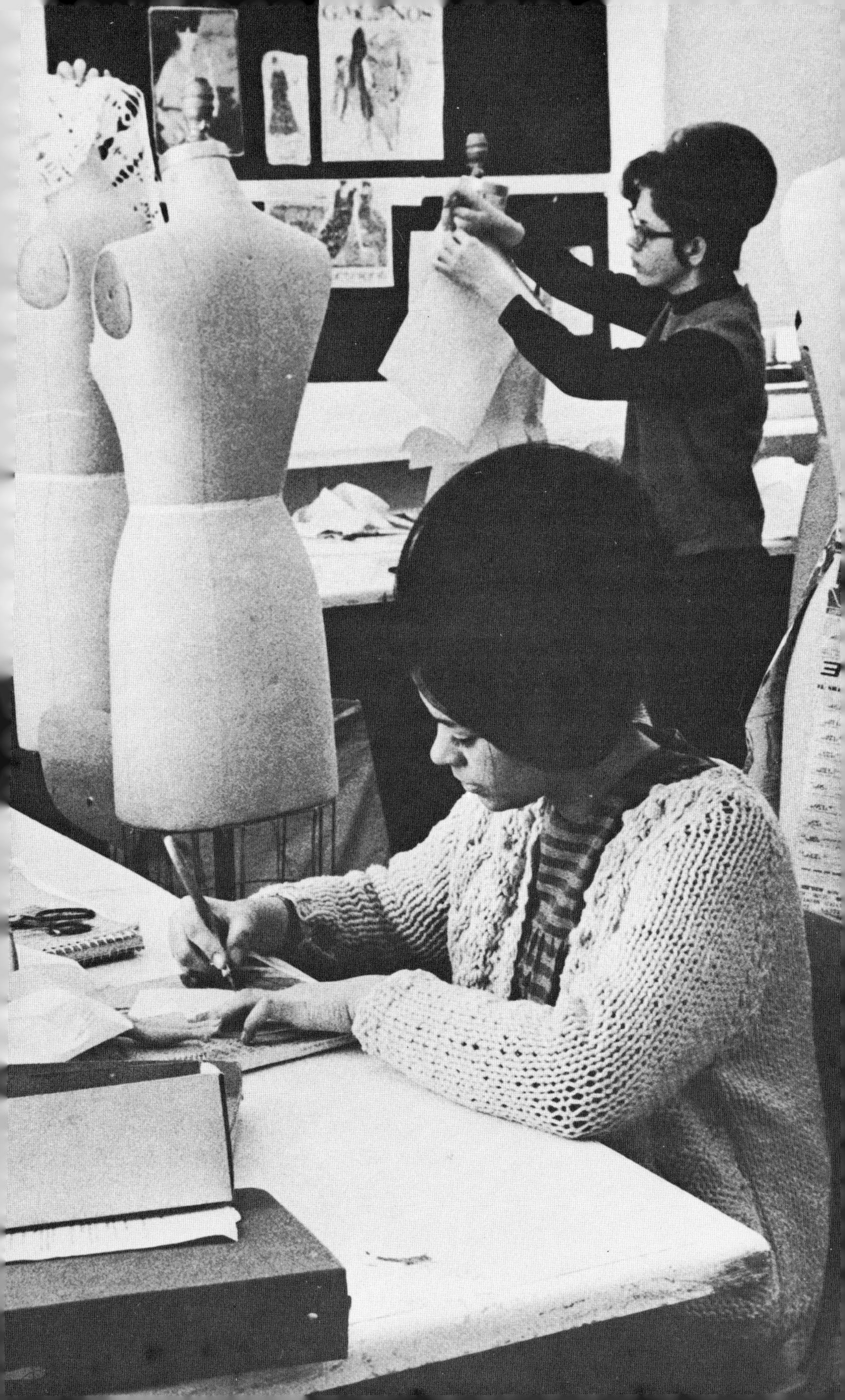

Without getting down to the nitty-gritty of design study, let us look at the way one designer works.

Helen Lee, a leading children's wear designer, will not employ anyone in her workroom who has ever worked for another manufacturer. She wants only fresh, untrained young people who have had two to four years of specialized schooling and whose desire is to design expressly for children.

For the first six months she expects very little in the way of results that can be used commercially. She wants her new employees to become familiar with fabrics, the look, the touch, the clothes. They are expected to learn to translate a style from size to size, until they develop a sense of proportion.

Other designers have other rules for the young people they hire, but most agree that a good general rule is to look at the world around you, to relate design to the times. Also, one must visit museums regularly, consult fashion histories, check on design sections of current publications.

For you who expect to go into design, the future is indeed exciting. You are taking part in all the advances in technology; you may even be dressing travelers to go to the moon.

You may be asked to design costumes to fit different environments from ours, so perhaps you will want to study physics and chemistry, as well as fashion.

You may have a chance to make disposable designs, like paper suits and dresses. Yours, however, will be more advanced, and your synthetics will have better wearing qualities than paper.

Maybe you will present to a waiting world garments

that light up and change colors as the lighting or temperature in a room changes. You may choose to weld metal or plastic links together to form clothing as has one very imaginative designer.

If far-out design does not interest you, perhaps you will combine science and design as your school major and initiate a new field. Who knows, you may use a computer and have it compute your designs just as it now renders works of art or comes up with new names for fabrics.

Any personal fantasy you want to make come true is within the realm of possibility. What an exciting field you are entering!

CHAPTER 9

It's a Model World
— or is it?

To MANY OF YOU the most glamorous job in the fashion world is modeling. You have visions of traveling the world over and being photographed in romantic places, draped in golden chains and silks and furs, tended by makeup men and fawned over by photographers.

What is the true story on modeling—what are the facts? The fact is that the number of young people planning a modeling career far exceeds the number of openings, but do not let that stop you. There is always room at the top.

If you have perfect grooming, easy poise, a pleasant personality, and also physical energy and lots of determination, you may make it.

In a recent article on models *Women's Wear Daily* pointed out that oddly enough, in this day when doing your own thing has become so important, it is still the same kind of beautiful girl that is wanted at the model agencies. She has long hair, a long neck, short nose, fringed eyes, a kissy mouth, good bones and a big bagful of "natural" cosmetics.

Still, there are signs of change. Naomi Sims, a black girl from Pittsburgh, came to New York a few years ago to study fashion merchandising — and earned sixty thousand dollars in one year as a model. "Be yourself" is the advice Naomi gives to young aspirants. "Let your own personality come through."

A girl of twenty-one can look forward to only about five years before the cameras, though there are always exceptions. Short-lived as the job may be, the *Occupational Outlook Quarterly* says there were fifty thousand persons engaged in modeling last year.

A small but growing percentage of models are male, and most models, male or female, specialize in some way, either in fashion or in photographic work. The best of them earn a very high hourly wage.

Fashion models may be employed by apparel designers, by manufacturers and wholesalers. They are then called showroom or wholesale models. Buyers from retail stores are shown the clothes quickly and effectively on the human figure, rather than on hangers or racks.

A fashion model, or mannequin, as she is sometimes called, wears clothing and accessories with grace. She has to walk, pivot, make back and side turns, so that buyers can see the merchandise from all angles. Some models point up the high fashion ideas in what they are wearing, and sometimes may give the style number and price of the item shown, so a good voice is an asset. Especially if you get into the really lucrative end, television commercials, where the fees keep coming for months or even years after the commercial is made, each time it is shown.

When the busy season is at hand, the model is always at work in the showroom, but she may perform clerical jobs in the slack or quiet season. (Here again the need to learn to type and develop clerical skills is illustrated. They will last long after looks have faded.)

Retail modeling for department stores, boutiques, specialty stores or custom salons (where clothes are made-to-order and are very expensive, usually) is generally conducted for customers and is more leisurely than in showrooms.

Often a designer from New York or California, or even from Paris or Rome, may bring his clothes to a certain store and have a "trunk" showing. He will need models to show his designs.

Often stores have special bridal showings, and here again free-lance models are needed.

FASHION SHOW MODELING

During fashion shows, which is what many of you envision when you think of modeling, details of the ensemble are described by the commentator and are shown at the same time by the model. Fashion show modeling is hectic, for the ability to change costumes quickly and still look glamorous and put-together is important. Usually you have less than five minutes to make a change, and even with backstage help, this is difficult.

Today, when multi-media, swinging presentations are important, a model may have to know how to dance her way along the runway, she may even have to sing or act a little. She will have to adjust to blinking strobe lights and other devices a producer may use.

Some fashion show models double as commentators, or they may produce shows themselves, especially after they gain experience. Photographic models also work for advertising or editorial employers. Here many special types, such as housewives, truck drivers or children, are needed.

For editorial features, the model's work is much like fashion photography, except that newspaper or magazine fashion editors use pictures to illustrate fashion news, the latest hair styles, apparel and accessories. This is hard and tiring work, but often pays very well.

Some models demonstrate new products and services at trade shows, in commercial or fashion films, or on television. Others stand for designers, who drape or fit their creations on them.

Here are some figures (that's a play on words) on the estimated fifty thousand models in the United States who worked last year. Many worked part-time, and four out of five were women or girls. The largest number worked in New York City, the center of the fashion industry, but large numbers also worked in Chicago, Dallas, Detroit, Los Angeles, Miami, and San Francisco.

Manufacturers, designers, and wholesalers employ the largest number of full time models. Many models also work for advertising agencies, retail stores, mail order houses, and magazines, as well as fashion illustrators.

HOW CAN A MODEL MODEL?

Naturally, you want to know how to get started in the field because most employers prefer models with

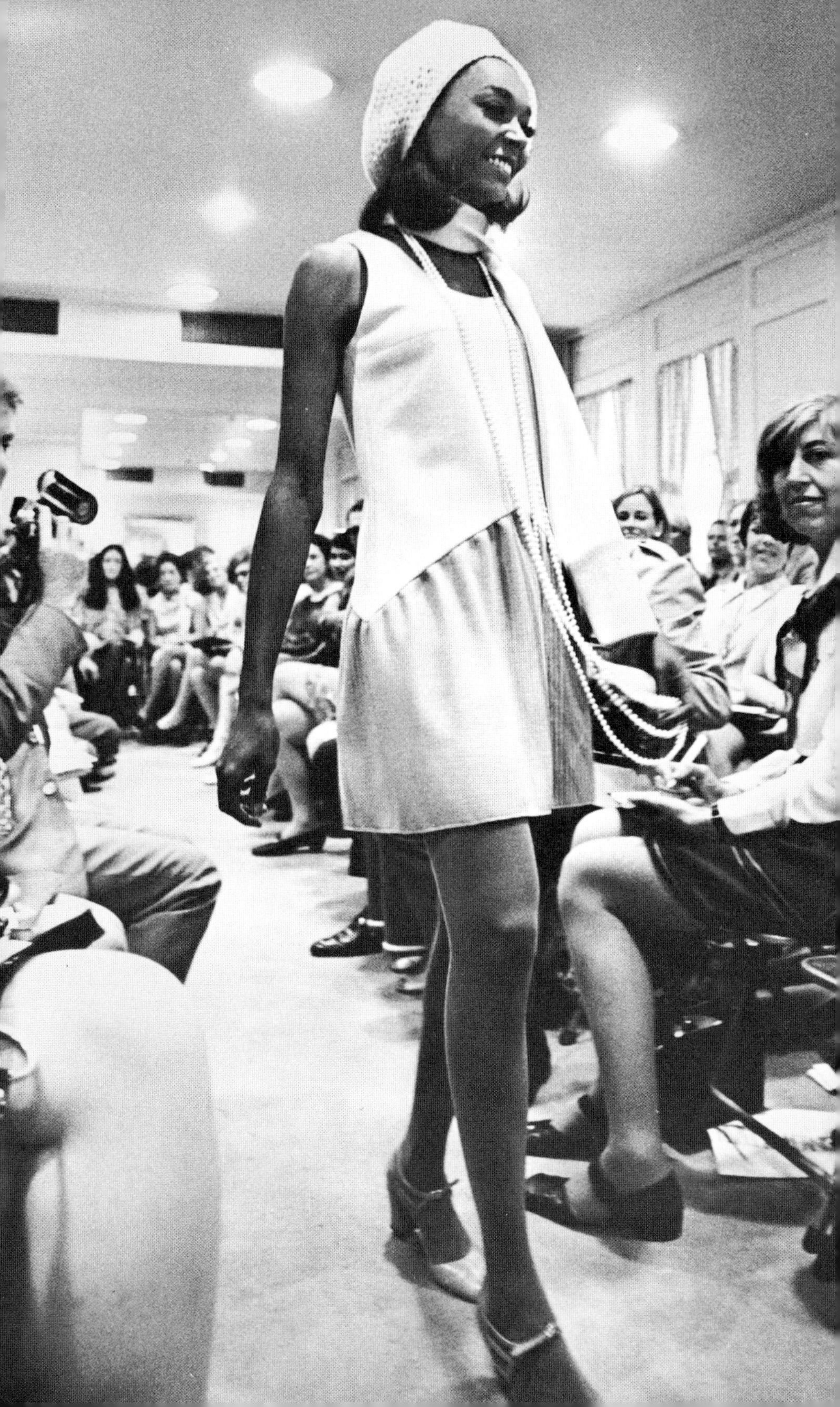

training or experience. One model got her first job by chance. (A photographer saw her and used her for a cover of a *New York Times* fashion supplement). But this model had trouble getting a second job until she got one hundred copies of the paper and sent them to one hundred art directors.

You could attend a reputable modeling or charm school to learn the right way to walk and stand, how to style your hair and use makeup, and to wear the clothes that are right for you.

Incidentally, even if you are not planning to model, a charm course is not a bad idea. It will give you poise and make meeting people and dating easier. Your best features will be pointed out to you, and you can then play them up. Your YWCA, YWHA or Community Center may offer such courses for a very small fee. Sometimes your 4H, Campfire or Girl Scout leader can tell you where to go for classes.

In a regular modeling school, you might attend a photographic modeling class, learning how to pose and how to change your facial expressions. Here again, sometimes you can do just as well without special training, but more often than not it will help.

Placement offices at modeling schools occasionally get students their first jobs, but don't count on this, though it may have been promised when you enrolled for your course. Some modeling schools are very honest, others are not quite so trustworthy, so don't be disappointed if you do not end up being another Twiggy on your first try. Incidentally, the famous young English model Twiggy never had a lesson.

Some lucky hopefuls get work by registering at a model agency. The agency usually asks you to have poses made to see the different ways you can look. These are arranged in a book and shown to people who might hire you.

Department stores sometimes have auditions to discover modeling talent. Also be sure to try out for store teen-boards, as we mentioned earlier, for here you nearly always will model back-to-school clothes on the floor, and perhaps in shows for students and their parents.

You might also get experience modeling in local charity fund-raising shows, or maybe your school or church is planning to put on a show.

EDUCATIONAL REQUIREMENTS

It is true you do not need formal education for many modeling jobs, and this may appeal to some of you. But again, remember that every business is getting tougher. Some employers want at least a high school diploma so you sound intelligent and literate if you talk to their customers.

Some people who hire models even require college training, and, certainly, courses in art, speech, drama, dancing, and even salesmanship can be useful. Remember those old reliables, typing and shorthand, too.

You young models must not only have a flair for style, but in most cases, be well-proportioned and slim. You might, however, model for manufacturers or stores that specialize in the short, the tall, and the stout. A shoe model must wear a size four or five, and a male model should be able to wear regular sizes, usually a forty regular suit. You are most often hired to fit the clothing; the clothes come first, not you.

If you like to work in front of the camera, remember

it makes you look ten to fifteen pounds heavier than you are, so slim and tall is the best way to be, for health and for beauty.

As was pointed out when we talked about fashion show modeling, modeling can serve as a stepping-stone to such jobs as fashion coordinator, editor on the staff of a fashion magazine or fashion consultant. Twiggy, for instance, has used her fame to lend her name to a large number of items, including ready-to-wear and eye lashes. A few models, who serve as doubles in movies or television, may become actresses. One lovely lady I know is now a television news announcer, but keeps up her fashion modeling, too. Some boys and girls work their way through art school by modeling and then are in a position to qualify as fashion illustrators.

YOUR CHANCES

Occupational Outlook Quarterly says full time modeling will remain very competitive through the 1970s, with most openings coming from those models who leave the field either because they are too old or because their faces have been seen too often. Many girls also decide to get married and raise families. For these reasons, eight years is usually tops for a girl, while a male model may last twenty years.

Manufacturers, wholesalers and retailers usually employ models on a permanent basis, although this is not always true.

Information on union memberships and regulations for television modeling can be obtained from local television stations or model agencies.

You can check on professional modeling schools and

charm schools by writing to the Department of Education in your state for approved schools. You can also check with the Better Business Bureau or Chamber of Commerce. Write the director of the school which interests you for tuition costs.

Incidentally, if you are interested in modeling, you may be interested in the findings of Dr. David P. Campbell, an associate professor of psychology at the University of Minnesota, and director of Center for Interest Measurement Research.

He asked one hundred famous fashion models in New York, Paris, and Minneapolis to take Strong Vocational Interest Blank tests, similar to what all of you will fill out as you get further in your schooling.

Here is what Dr. Campbell discovered, and he tells it in his own words: "First, fashion models tend to develop exaggerated ideas of their own worth, and this is quite understandable. Anyone who is paid up to sixty dollars or eighty dollars an hour just to stand still, and then has her face and figure, looking her very best, splashed coast-to-coast on the covers of the most prestigious magazines, can hardly be expected to keep both feet firmly on the ground. Some of them, to their very great credit, manage to. For others, the problems are great. A few, fifteen years old and making thirty-five thousand dollars a year, become high school dropouts; a substantial number of them later have trouble making marriages work.

Well, there is the model story, the good and the bad. Good luck to all you beautiful young people who think you might want to take the plunge.

CHAPTER 10

The Excitement of the Marketplace —Retailing

RETAILING AND MERCHANDISING are two areas all of you know about even if you know very little about other parts of the fashion business. After all, each of you is a consumer (one who consumes or uses goods) and each of you goes to a store to buy merchandise.

If you have entered a hobby shop to buy a model airplane you have visited a retailer. If you have walked into a fabric store to buy wool for a jumper you plan to sew, you have been to a retail establishment. When you visit the corner hardware, grocery or drugstore, you have seen a retailer.

Come to think of it, you could do all of the above errands in one large department store, and you would have visited a different kind of retailer.

Perhaps you prefer to save every penny you can so you do all your buying at a discount store, where service is kept at a minimum so that overhead (the fixed cost of running a business) is kept low. A discount store is another kind of retailing, as is the franchise store. Maybe you have heard of Paraphernalia or Villager. These apparel stores use a registered and well-known name and pay the owner of the name for the privilege. They also get help in running the store from the franchise owner. But more on franchising later.

We could make out lists of things which are bought from some kind of store; many would contain fashion merchandise, many would not. Unless we are farmers or other home producers, we must buy what we need from some kind of retailer or merchandiser. Before we go on talking about department stores, discount stores, boutiques, specialty stores, and franchisers, we might mention some other ways merchandise can be bought.

You could, if you wished, order all your choices by mail or telephone from a catalogue of a mail order firm such as Sears Roebuck or Montgomery Ward, or others in that field. You could also choose from an advertisement in a newspaper or magazine, or even from a television or radio advertisement. In radio these are called "spots" or "spot announcements."

If you keep up with these things you may have heard that someday there will be special television channels attached to your set that will make it possible for you to push a button and have articles of merchandise flashed on the screen. An operator will tell you the available colors and sizes, the prices, and the delivery date. You can see what you buy without ever leaving home.

This would be a marvelous assist for shut-ins or for those who are too busy to shop. I, for one, hope I will always be able to walk into an exciting boutique or other shop and do my choosing "live." It is one of the pleasures of our times. Anyhow, if one is not careful one can become the slave of the machine instead of the master.

Besides, the stores and shops of the '70s have become so exciting architecturally with their creative uses of lighting and sculptural display areas that one would not want to miss the fun. It is the same excitement one gets from visiting a wonderful museum show or a theater, and there is the added pleasure of being able to buy what is shown. Who would want to miss the crazy "shops within shops" with rock music and light shows. All this and merchandise, too.

Advising a sales promotion executives group recently, David Yunich, head of Macy's, one of the major stores in the country, told them to be prepared for changes in the methods of merchandise presentation in the future.

He said, "The merchant will be more of a showman than he is today, more creative, more innovative, more concerned with how he presents his message. Rather than a buyer-and-seller, rather than a department manager, tomorrow's merchant will be an impressario."

By the time the next century arrives, the merchant will be responsible "not only for moving merchandise, but in creating it as well," Yunich said.

The executive display director of Saks Fifth Avenue, Henry Callahan, earlier told the same group that, "I would love to live to see that shopping was as much fun as going to Coney Island was in the old days or to Disneyland today."

Mr. Callahan feels that with people so attuned to

realism by their constant exposure to television, the shopping center of the future will be a "fantasy land" where fun and practicability will combine to make shopping a delight.

Before we get too carried away with the visual delights of retailing and merchandising, let us get back to definitions.

The Random House Dictionary of the English Language has a great definition of "merchandising." It says: "The planning and promotion of sales by presenting a product to the right market at the proper time, by carrying organized, skillful advertising, using attractive displays, etc. Also called 'merchandise planning'."

Nothing could be made more clear than that. As for "retail," the same source says it is simply "the sale of goods to ultimate consumers, usually in small quantities (opposed to wholesale)."

Having developed our base, let us remember retailing and merchandising go hand-in-hand, and, though some of you may have never thought about it that way, retailing is a most adventurous and romantic kind of profession. Also you can make it big while you are still young.

Retailers come in all sizes and shapes with all kinds of educations, though the better-educated usually make it to the top faster.

Many men and women who trained in other fields have become legendary figures in retailing. The famous Rich's of Atlanta, for more than a quarter of a century, had a man as president who started out as an engineer.

John Wanamaker, first of the famous retailing clan, knew as a child that he wanted to own a store and he dedicated himself to that idea.

Several executives of the Dayton Hudson Corporation are teachers at heart. Sam Druy, a Phi Beta Kappa (most of you know that this is a high scholastic honor) from Brown University, is one of that conglomerate's top executives, heading its jewelry division. He has, however, worked in many phases of retailing and found them all exciting. He likes to lecture to young people eager to go into the retailing field, and hopes one day, upon reaching retirement age, to become a college lecturer and share his know-how with many of you.

He recently gave some interesting and relevant facts to a group of students attending the St. Paul-Minneapolis Fashion Group's career course, which was swingingly, if ungrammatically, entitled, "Fashion Biz—Like It Is!"

He explained that retailing is one of the few fields where you test your knowledge almost daily, and where you can tell almost immediately if you have made the right choices. A buyer who has made errors must live with his or her mistakes — only they are called "markdowns." A retailer can experiment with display, with a new selling approach, with almost anything.

Mr. Druy points out that with the coming of the computer a new excitement has come into retailing. He says, "Now you can literally program your hunches and see if they pay off." He says that 90 percent of the merchandise used by one division of the Dayton Hudson Corporation is programmed and the firm wants an even higher percentage of purchases programmed in this manner.

He is careful to point out, however, that a successful programmer must be creative, competitive and imaginative. The machine is still the servant of the man or woman.

The importance of youth in retailing is made clear in some figures Mr. Druy gave to the career group. He said the Dayton stores have 20 percent of their buyers under the age of twenty-eight and that half the merchandise men are under thirty-five. The average age of a Dayton vice president is forty-four. These figures vary in other companies in other parts of the country, but everywhere the emphasis is on youth.

Also remember the term "retailing" takes in an operation like Neiman Marcus in Dallas, noted for its expensive and unusual merchandise, as well as such mail-order giants as Sears Roebuck and Montgomery Ward.

Stanley Marcus, the guiding genius of Neiman-Marcus, was asked in a recent interview what he had done to attract young people into retailing. He answered that his firm recruited at twenty-seven different colleges, that they sponsored college lectures and had an executive training program lasting two months.

He noted that it has always been a problem finding the right young people but pointed out that that is not exclusively a retailing problem. He said, "There's a people shortage for the pace of our whole economy."

We have been using terms such as "buyer," "merchandiser," and "vice president" without really explaining them. In a sense they are self-explanatory. The buyer buys merchandise which sales people must sell. The merchandise man or woman works with figures, decides what percentages of each kind of merchandise the buyer will stock, after discussing the matter with the buyer. One merchandiser can have many buyers in his or her "division." Thus a merchandiser of men's apparel departments may have under him the neckwear buyer, the better suit buyer, the accessories buyer, the boys' wear buyer, the coat buyer, and so on. A vice president usually heads a group, including buyers and merchandisers or he may be an advertising or public relations vice president or a vice president handling the real estate part of a retail establishment or conglomerate.

Remember that selling is a good way to start up the managerial ladder.

THE ROMANCE OF RETAILING

Now, let us talk a little about the romance of retailing and about its history. Tom Jeglosky, a Dayton Hudson corporate official in communications, and another Phi Beta Kappa, is a former teacher who is fascinated with the history of buying. He says that for centuries, whether Viking, Saxon, Latin, Russian, or American — men have encouraged and sponsored expeditions and inquiries. Far-off lands have been explored and the secrets of science or society have been probed. Men have been encouraged to find things out, to bring back the new and the different and the useable, the colorful and the strong, the interesting and the informative.

Sometimes the data from these expeditions comes back in the form of scientific knowledge, but think of how often it has returned instead in the form of saleable merchandise. Raleigh brought back maize and tobacco, but he also brought back mother-of-pearl and blueberry paints.

And how about one of the great explorers of all time, Marco Polo? He was a merchant who sought the profitable new technique and the profitable product with which he could return to Venice, assume leadership of his family and make his own fortune greater.

Marco Polo really brought home more ideas than merchandise, and that again is why merchandising can be so satisfying, why retailing can be more than a business.

Many retailers I talked to pointed out that someone interested in merchandising must have individuality as did those early searchers for the goods of the world.

Management is always looking for people who can spot the trend that creates fresh thinking.

So, what are we saying? Merely that a retailer today can be like the adventurer of old who finds the life style we all want through goods and products. Instead of going in an ancient wooden vessel, however, todays' adventurer hops a jet, or a taxi or a luxury ship (time permitting) and searches out the world's treasures.

Before we end the chapter, let us again make clear that retailing takes many forms. We talked about the many kinds of stores which exist, and about franchising, the newest form of retailing.

Franchising is probably the most rapidly growing form of business organization in the United States.

In 1967 it included an estimated eleven thousand franchising companies and four hundred thousand franchised businesses, accounting for some ninety billion dollars in annual sales.

Although many franchised operations are not in the fashion field, a goodly number are. Paraphernalia and Villager Industries are two examples. One department store chain is even involved in a fried chicken "takeout" enterprise.

We have been talking about the history of retailing, which really goes back to the first day two humans decided to exchange wares. Maybe one needed an animal skin and traded it for a piece of wood. That moment has not been set down for us historically, but we can imagine it. Barter was the beginning of retailing. Remember, beads bought Manhattan Island.

But while we are talking about all the good things in retailing and merchandising, we must remember, too, "the dark side of the marketplace." That is also the title of a book by Senator Warren G. Magnuson and Jean Carper, as well as a comment on our forefathers and what they did to the Indians to get Manhattan. These two authors tell us all about buying and selling and about the concern there has always been for you and me, the consumers. But they point out that there have always been some unscrupulous people who did not tell the truth about their wares. Even in the Middle Ages, public servants had to worry and see to it their people were not cheated, although all goods were displayed in the open market and could be examined thoroughly for defects.

The situation became worse for consumers over the centuries, but in the past few years great advances have been made in helping us. There are food and drug acts and labeling acts and many other laws to help. The 1960s were called the "decade of the consumer" because so much was done to protect us against misleading information and deceitful practices.

The 1970s promise even more needed reform.

We could go on and on with this chapter on retailing, for the resources are endless. Instead, let us go on to the following chapter for the breakdown of the various jobs in retailing we have not covered adequately so far.

CHAPTER 11

A Store is Many Things — and Many People

OUR LAST CHAPTER gave broad definitions of retailing and of merchandising. Once, however, you have decided that your future in fashion will definitely be in a store—department, boutique, specialty or discount—where do you go from there?

You could go anywhere, from stock boy or girl to store president or chairman of the board. Many others have, before you. But, first, face the facts of merchandising life. If you are a clock-watcher, forget retailing. There are no such things as regular hours. During holiday and other peak seasons, the hours are long.

Should you become a buyer or merchandiser, you will have to dash off to fashion showings in the men's, women's, children's, home or allied fields. Sometimes these showings begin early in the morning (if you are lucky they serve you breakfast at the show) and can go on to the wee hours. (I attended a very glamorous affair once in formal attire and was not even served a glass of water although the showing ran nearly to midnight.)

Showings are just a small, if exciting, part of retailing life. You must plan on training meetings, advertising meetings, department conferences, and even extra schooling on your own time as well as store time.

As you go up the fashion retailing ladder, there may be much traveling. True, it may be glamorous on occasion, but it is also time-consuming, and often frustrating. Even if your travels up to now have been limited to going with your family or on student tours, you know the waiting and the foul-ups that can occur as more and more people go more and more places and the jets get more jumbo.

And always, no matter what part of retailing you choose, you must be charming, accessible, and make your customers feel welcome. You must ply them with services. No temper, no tantrums, and no backtalk, even though you as a customer may not always have had it so good from those who were serving you. In theory at least, the customer is always right. Stop and think how you resented it, maybe you even decided not to go back to the store whose employee was rude to you. That is how others feel, too.

You can understand that you, in turn, cannot be rude if you want your store to be successful and make a success of you.

The career of fashion buying, should you choose it, is a varied one. There are many departments, and many areas, but whichever you choose the field demands good sense, good taste, and good humor.

If you are very enthusiastic about your career, and if you have or can raise the capital to get started, buying

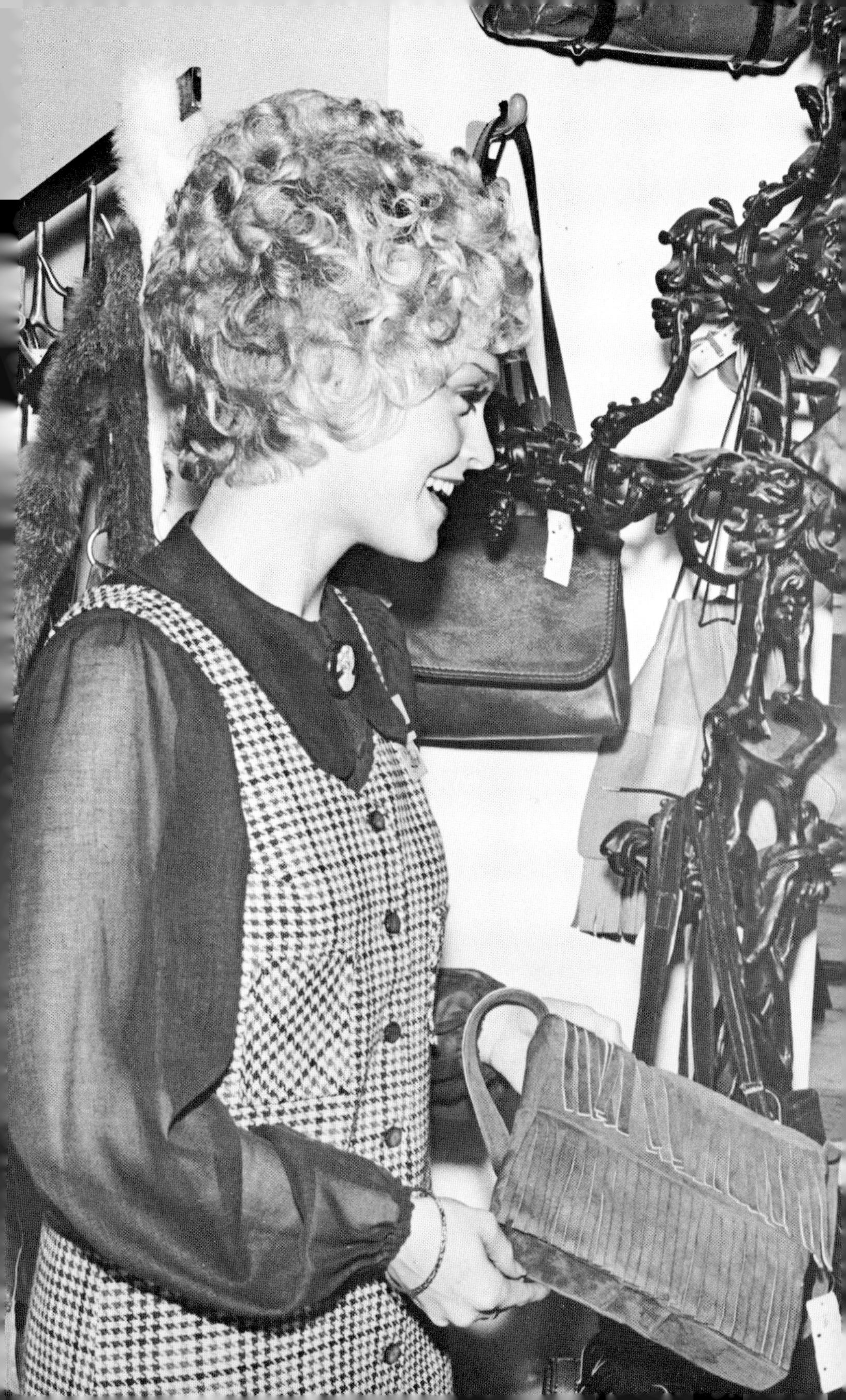

can lead to having your own business. Also, here is a career that can go on indefinitely. Although the emphasis these days is on youth and you can hit the top quickly, you can also go on into your middle and older years. As you get older, what you lack in exuberance, you will make up in knowledge and culture.

As a buyer in the fashion arena, you must keep up with the times — politically, socially, economically, every way possible. Read all the trade and consumer publications you can, and make the scene. Live the way many of your customers do so you can understand their needs.

When you buy, you must choose items that may not necessarily appeal to you, but will appeal to others. Everything is not for you. A big girl must think small if she buys for a junior department. A tall, handsome young man must think short and fat if he buys for a special size men's department. Ego is good, but personal likes must be put aside when you hope to sell to a lot of people those items you have bought.

No matter at what level of retailing you begin, remember all along the way to be kind and look down on no one! Everyone who has ever read a book on basic selling knows that the customer with the biggest diamonds and the most furs is not always the wealthiest or the most willing to buy.

My mother, Madame Jeanne Auerbacher, who was famed in her day as the buyer for a very glamorous high fashion department, the Oval Room at Dayton's, always told her sales personnel to treat all customers alike and give them undivided attention. Occasionally however, one of the ladies took herself rather seriously and ignored a customer who did not look as if she "belonged."

One day a rather forlorn little woman in a baggy coat and dress to match, waited in vain for an Oval Room sales person to wait on her. Mother came out of her office, noticed the customer, inquired into her needs and sold her thousands of dollars worth of merchandise — coats, suits, dresses, hats, the works. The woman was a mining heiress from a small town in the Dakotas and came to Minneapolis once a year to get a complete wardrobe. And so it goes.

Store advertising or publicity is very much like working in a large advertising agency. You must be highly organized and have an ability to write and to create ideas. Again, you must know the ways of the typewriter and other sophisticated machines and you must be able to deal with other store personnel. Much of this we covered in our fashion writing and advertising chapters. Also there are many good books on the subject, for instance, Bernice Fitz-Gibbon's, *Macy's, Gimbels, and Me.*

Miss Fitz-Gibbon is the lady who revolutionized department store advertising and ended up earning ninety thousand dollars a year. Many of her slogans have become legends in the department store world.

Miss Fitz-Gibbon still loves writing copy after all these years. She says advertising creates wants, and nudges and nags people to get a hustle on and satisfy those wants. She finds that fitting and proper, and so will you if you chose advertising and publicity.

These days you will also be in show business if you choose this field. You will book talent and work with celebrities and handle movies and cooking schools and sewing schools and fashion shows and heaven knows what else. It's hectic, but fun.

Also part of publicity, but perhaps parallel to it, are fashion coordination and shows. If you are a fashion coordinator for a store, you may well go to the New York, California, and European markets to anticipate fashion trends. Then you will preview these trends for your store personnel as well as for customers. You may advise buyers on how much merchandise to have, what kind, and how soon.

You will assist your store display people in their choices for interior and window display, because this must be done well in advance of the season. You will help promote your store's progressive image by your choices. Will your store think young, will it be a leader, will it appeal to the community's needs? All these things will be partly in your hands.

Besides viewing fashions in advance and presenting them, you may also help coordinate retail stocks in various departments, and approve fashion releases and photos sent out by the publicity department to newspapers and magazines and trade publications.

You may commentate your store's fashion shows at country clubs, service clubs or other places. You will work closely with your training department and keep them hep on matters of fashion.

When your store plans big advertising or in-store promotions, you will be there along with all the advertising, merchandising and promotion personnel to make the promotion pay off in prestige and sales.

As a beginner, you can start anywhere in a store and make your way as you go along. Some jobs include: advertising, alterations, clerical work, corporate office work, credit interviewing, data processing, display, gift wrapping, maintenance, merchandise handling, sales, modeling, personnel, payroll, receiving, receptionist, sales manager, secretary, ticket office, and management. Some stores even have travel bureaus and insurance departments—any and all can lead to something big if you are sharp enough and smart enough to make yourself noticed. If you are a skier, you may work in the ski shop. If tennis is of more interest to you, work in the sports equipment and accessories department. Use your hobby to aid you in your job.

Stores offer fringe benefits such as hospitalization, sick leave, life insurance, paid vacations, and holidays as well as employee discounts.

SELL, SELL, SELL

Lots of fashion greats started by selling. It is a great way to know human nature—yours and other people's! Besides, the success of any retail business depends on its salespeople. You know that clerks sell, but what else do they do? They make out sales or charge slips, get cash payments and give change and receipts. They also handle returns and exchange of merchandise. They usually help keep their work areas neat and in smaller stores may help in ordering merchandise, stacking shelves or racks, marking price tags, taking inventories, and preparing displays and promoting sales in other ways.

As you have noticed from the above, a good sales person can be almost anything in a store and can learn many facets of the business along the way.

Time for a few figures again. Nearly 2.9 million salespersons—nearly three-fifths of them women—were employed in early 1967, in close to one hundred different kinds of retail businesses.

As for educational requirements, employers generally prefer high school graduates who took courses in salesmanship, commercial arithmetic, and home economics.

We are back to the old pleasing personality, the neat appearance and the ability to communicate clearly, as well as an interest in sales work.

We must not forget the salesmen who work for wholesale outlets and manufacturers. For them, the pay is much higher than for store salespeople and the qualifications are also higher. More than 550 thousand salespeople, 95 percent of them men, worked for wholesalers in 1967.

Unmentioned so far, too, are the thousands of workers in retail buying offices. Big retail chains have their own offices in New York and around the world to check the markets and to buy in quantity for all their stores. Some small stores band together and pay for their own buying offices. Thus they get the advantages a large combine achieves. The buyers here are similar to store buyers, but they also act as hosts and hostesses for store personnel and management when they come to the city. They also send weekly newsletters to member stores.

Store display is another good starting place for a creative boy or girl. Many art school and design school students work part-time in display, and several I know free-lance in that field for small shops to earn tuition. Some of the biggest names in retailing began in display.

These days when many stores have suburban branches and branches in other cities, a creative person interested in architecture can find a career as a store architect. He or she can also be a free-lance architect or have a firm and specialize in the fashion retailing field. Many have made great names for themselves designing shopping centers all over the country.

Retailing, as we said before, offers endless possibilities. Somewhere there is a place for you. It may even be in a new franchise operation, first started in Europe, which claims it will be the first to see new items as they come on the market and as soon as the new item is sold, the owners are pledged to go on to something else. All the sales personnel, it is said, will be groovy, pretty, and courteous . . . courteous above all!

CHAPTER 12

The Manufacturer is All — and Then Some

OK, SO NOW YOU KNOW how to sell fashion, how to write about it, and how to advertise it. You can design it and you can model it, but who makes it and who makes it all possible? The manufacturer, of course.

He or she or they (some manufacturers have many partners or many businesses, for that matter) employ over a million and a half workers just to make clothing for this nation's population. The apparel industry produces about ninety dollars worth of clothing annually for every man, woman and child. And that does not even include all the accessories that go along with being "dressed."

Naturally, this manufacturing industry is an important job source for people with widely different skills and interests. Some jobs can be learned in a few weeks; others take years.

Did you know that the apparel industry is the nation's largest employer of women in manufacturing? Four out of five garment workers are women, and most of them work as sewing machine operators.

There are many other jobs for women such as those we discussed earlier as well as those, for instance, of hand sewer or bookkeeper. Men usually hold down such jobs as cutter, marker, presser, production manager, engineer, and salesman. We will not go into the job of designer here because we gave it a whole chapter earlier. Remember, though, that a talented designer can make or break a firm if it is known as a creative house. Copyists and low mark-up manufacturers can get along without a designer by merely adapting fashions already on the market.

It would be easy at this point to give miles of figures on how many men and women work in each part of the apparel industry, but you would be bored. Let us say the nearly a million and a half men and women who worked in the apparel industries in 1967 made dresses, skirts, blouses and suits for women, girls and children. They produced tailored clothing, including suits, overcoats, topcoats and sportcoats for men and boys. Also they turned out men's and boy's shirts, slacks, work clothes, separate trousers, nightwear, undergarments, and other furnishings.

Can you think of other items of apparel we skipped? How about caps, hats, and other millinery? Then there are undergarments for women and children, fur goods, rain coats, gloves and dressing gowns and other at-home wear. Again, let us not forget the bridal industry. It is big business, as is knitwear.

And we did not even mention all kinds of adornments and accessories, but they count, too, especially now with vests of chains and even metal breast-plates being worn, as well as six-foot long necklaces and scarfs.

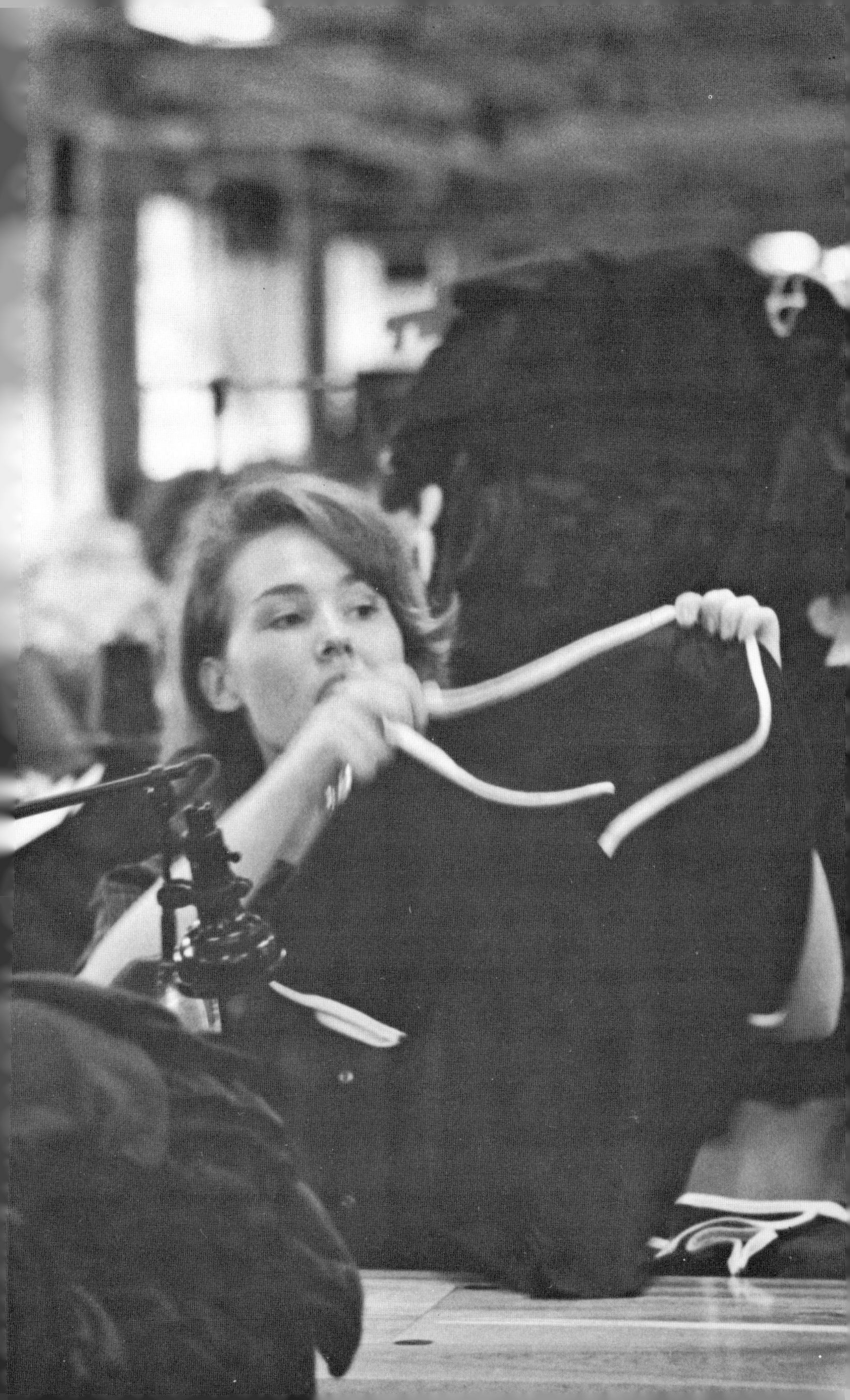

Although there has been a trend toward larger factories, most wholesale establishments are still small, with a handful employing a thousand or more people. Usually one hundred employees or less work in a particular firm.

By now you all know that New York is the nation's garment center, although apparel factories are located in nearly every state. Most large firms, no matter where they have a home base, maintain a sales office in New York to make it easier for store buyers to view their latest styles. This is especially true for high fashion merchandise.

In the men's field, now becoming with it, the Middle Atlantic region has the largest group of factories. The *New York Times* recently called the increase in men's wear interest the "peacock revolution" and said it was caused by the fact that men had more money to spend on themselves.

The newspaper pointed out that the average family income approached ten thousand dollars in 1968 and that men are able to spend more, but it is probably the population increase that is most responsible for increased sales.

Really the fact that designs have become more exciting, that color has become important and that new fabrics, like knits, are becoming big, has made men's wear even more important. Also, men are becoming more adventurous. Look at all the colored shirts they're wearing, as just one example.

Talking about knitwear brings up another kind of manufacturing—the fabric maker. We must think of all the makers of cotton, rayon and other synthetics, silk, wool, blends. Then there are the various makers of thread and trims and knit fabrics and all those people who manufacture the various processes by which fabrics are made wrinkleproof, no-iron and non-shrink, as well as non-fade. It has been said the five billion dollar knitwear industry in America will account for 75 percent of all women's wearing apparel within the next five years.

We could go on and on explaining the various jobs and processes in apparel manufacturing but again, turn to the Department of Commerce pamphlets for the facts and figures. Just remember that the manufacturing segment of fashion has a niche for almost everyone.

DO YOUR OWN THING

I would like to add one thought. Perhaps some of you feel that you must go into a profession like the law or medicine because your parents wish it, but you feel you might be happier working with your hands. Consider going to a vocational school and becoming a tailor or furrier, for instance. These trades are dying out because so few young people go into them—yet, if your hands are quick and your head is not for legal or medical terms, why not consider becoming tops in this creative area? A good cutter or dresser or tailor can make excellent money, will always be sought after, and probably will end up being a firm owner, if he or she has stick-to-it power. An unhappy doctor or lawyer may make a parent happy, but how about himself?

In our own family this happened, but the story had a happy ending. My sister-in-law always wanted to work with her hands, either sewing or drawing or embroidering. Her parents decreed each child had to be a doctor, lawyer or pharmacist because that was the immigrant's dream for his children. Well, my sister-in-law became a pharmacist, a great profession IF you like it, and always made good money standing on her feet and dispensing pills.

Then, on her fiftieth birthday, she rebelled. You see, that generation rebelled later than yours. She quit pharmacy, opened a needlepoint boutique, and her little shop has become the most in place in town. Also, she is making a small fortune. She added precious jewelry to her needlepoint line and all the ladies in town flock to her shop to sew and buy and buy and sew. So much for pills vs. handwork.

Before we leave manufacturing, just a note on the fact that many small and many large, important manufacturers have been bought up by conglomerates or just by other manufacturers. For instance, a giant company like Genesco has in its fold many apparel and accessory firms, as well as retail outlets like Bonwit Teller, Henri Bendel and Tiffany. A milling firm, like General Mills, can own a big manufacturer of womenswear and menswear like David Crystal, and also have a jewelry firm like Monet. And so it goes. In your time this will happen more and more. Many manufacturers will become part of a big whole, others will manage to stay small and unique. If you go into this field, you will find it fascinating—and ever-changing.

You will find that many top designers are also entrepreneurs (better look that word up, too). A designer may be an owner in one company, and still design for many firms. He may have other designers working with him, as do many top design names who own their companies.

Oftentimes, a designer makes such a success of his

specialty that his boss, in order to keep his services—and his name—will give him a percentage of the manufacturing firm. Sometimes, but rarely, the designer will also turn out to be a good businessman, as at-home with financial figures as with human figures.

CHAPTER 13

And We Have Not Mentioned...

FASHION IS REALLY frustrating, especially when one tries to be logical about it. We have attempted to mention all the categories. Then, suddenly, here is the last chapter. BUT . . .

Nothing has been written about the beauty business, that multi-billion dollar part of fashion that includes all kinds of men's and women's cosmetics, hairstyling, suntan lotions and deodorants and false eyelashes and whatnot. You can get cosmetics at the department store, at the beauty salon, through the mail, door-to-door, and every which way. The beauty business is fabulous and fascinating, and you can make a career of it through chemistry, through journalism and advertising, through design, or through beauty school. Somebody made it big in each of these ways.

Nothing has been said about all the great fashion design laboratories and museums throughout the country. How about the Metropolitan Museum, the Brooklyn Museum, and the Philadelphia Museum, for starters? Also there are the Wordsworth Atheneum and the Dallas Merchandise Mart, with its own fashion gallery. There are many more, too.

True, we mentioned all along that you should visit museums as much as possible and see the old and the new art of all kinds, and we could add that your local historical society usually has great period costumes tucked away, as, occasionally, does the local Salvation Army. In fact, now there are flea market shops that stock great period attire and it can be bought, usually at not too wild a price. Start your own museum.

Some of you may want to specialize in fashion work in a museum and become curators.

Your best bet is a liberal education, with a heavy dose of art history, perhaps even a master's degree in art history. But you could get started just as well from the journalism field or from textile design, perhaps even from manufacturing. Fashion curator in a museum is a profession that has not been too well explored and should become more important as we try harder and harder to preserve fashion as a vital part of our history.

I pondered writing a full chapter on "art in fashion," but decided against it, as that is really another book.

So as for the age-old question, is fashion art? It is. And what is more, much of today's art is merely passing fashion.

You will note that when newspapers write about an art exhibit opening, they often spend as much time telling you who-wore-what as they do describing who-painted-what.

Nothing has been said about *home furnishings* as part of the fashion field. Here again design is all-important, as are color and fabric. Whatever we said about training for fashion goes for home furnishings. A knowledge of carpentry and manufacturing are great assets here; the sales background the same perhaps, as for fashion, except that more males sell in this field.

Nothing has been said about *photography,* although it was included as part of design training. Lots of talented young people in the modeling and other fashion fields work as photographers' assistants, helping with props, lighting, and all the other things involved in photography. Fashion photographers are among the most highly paid and most sought after photographers in the country.

Nothing has been said about *working part-time.* Many of you, after finishing school, or after working a few years, will settle down to marriage and raising families.

When your children are in school, you will be delighted to be able to go back to work. If fashion is your career, there are many places you can work part-time as well as full time. Selling is one area, but part-time publicity and advertising are in demand, as are models and even designers.

Remember fashion is for all-time, but it can also be great for part-time, for both men and women.

THE END

> But for you,
>   a fashionable beginning.

Quiz Yourself

Here are some questions to ask yourself. If you can answer "yes" to more than ten, you are probably meant to be somewhere in the fashion field—if fashion is what you want.

Do you like to keep up on all that is news in fashion?

Do you look to see what others are wearing?

Do you enjoy shopping for your own clothes, rather than having it done for you?

Do you like to help shop for your friends?

Do others ask your advice on what they should wear, or how they should do their hair?

Do you enjoy making your own clothes?

Do you like to work with your hands?

Do you enjoy visiting museums?

Do you do anything about decorating your own room?

Do you enjoy putting together decorations for parties or club events?

Do you like to handle publicity for your club or group?

Do you enjoy speaking before an audience?

Do you like to walk through department stores and specialty shops just to browse?

Do you remember prices of apparel you buy?

Do you compare prices to be sure you are getting the most for your money?

Do you enjoy being in plays or operettas?

Do you enjoy writing, either for your school paper, or as part of a club or other group activity?

Do you ever visit model rooms in furniture departments?

Are you a leader in your group?

Do you enjoy meeting groups of people?

Are you experimental in your way of dressing?

Are you happy if you are doing something creative?

Do you notice costumes in plays and movies?

Do you check to see who the costume and set designers are when you go to a play or movie?

Do you read fashion stories and columns in your local paper?

Do you regularly read any fashion magazines?

Perhaps some of you are now so interested in fashion you would like to read more books on the subject. Your school librarian or teacher will help you find other good books on fashion. The author of this book suggests the following:

ADAMS, J. DONALD	*Naked We Came*
BEATON, CECIL	*The Glass of Fashion*
BURT, OLIVE	*John Wanamaker, Boy Merchant*
KOLODNY, ROSALIE	*Fashion Designs for Moderns*
MERRIAM, EVE	*The Business of Being in Fashion*

Later on you may be interested in schools that specialize in fashion, or in finding more pamphlets and books on the subject. Your teacher, school librarian, or counselor will be able to provide valuable assistance.